the
forever
haze
of *after*

MY STORY OF RESILIENCE, STRENGTH, AND
COMPANIONSHIP WHILE NAVIGATING **MY AFTERS**

Hilary Marsh

For More Information, please visit
www.TheForeverHazeOfAfter.com
or contact Hilary at
TheForeverHazeOfAfter@gmail.com

Paperback ISBN: 978-1-7364410-0-8
E-book ISBN: 978-1-7364410-1-5
Library of Congress Control No: 2021900118

Website Design by A Slice of PR, Inc. (www.asliceofpr.com)
Cover Design by 100Covers.com

Interior Formatting by Nola Li Barr (Tapioca Press)
Photography by Suzie Ferro (www.SuzieFerro.com)

This book is dedicated to:
My mom, grandma, and brother Brock
My best friends
My BioFamily
My Uncle Rory
My husband, Andrew
And all the couples struggling with addiction

CONTENTS

INTRODUCTION

Every person has experienced a moment that changed them forever. Whether it was positive or negative, when it happened, you were never the same as you were just one second before. The Forever Haze of *After* is the realm you enter after that moment.

I have had a lot of those moments.

Imagine that right when your life is about to start at 13 years old, you find out your parents are divorcing. Imagine going from a seemingly normal family to a family full of police encounters and restraining orders. Imagine being at a party with all your friends, and then five minutes later, one of them is gone forever. Imagine finding a best friend out of tragedy. Imagine falling in love with a man you met when you were 12, and then finding out he's a heroin addict just as you're starting your love story. Imagine being told at 20 years old, after years of a tumultuous relationship, that your dad is actually not your dad. Imagine searching for your biological father for a decade and then, out of the blue, finding him—and eight siblings.

I never imagined any of these things could happen. But they happened. And when they did, each one changed my life—and put me into another "after."

I started keeping a diary after the first of my forever moments. I wrote daily for over 10 years. As the years went by, I always said I would write a book. Friends, seeing my life story play out, urged me to. I have tried to start this book many times before. Those times were not the right times.

Now, almost 20 years after the first entry in my diary, I feel such a sense of resolution. So much of what I am about to share has come full circle. The world is in an unprecedented state; the coronavirus has taken over and everything is shut down. Literally forced to stay at home, I can no longer say I don't have the time to do this.

Writing this book was as painful as it was healing. Reading some of my diary entries from when I was younger shed so much light on what I was going through internally. Throughout the first half of the book I will include diary excerpts to realistically express what I was feeling and thinking at those exact moments in time. I cleaned up the grammar and spelling errors that filled my diary, and some names have been changed for privacy. Other than that, the entries are as I wrote them at the time.

This is my story of resilience, strength, and companionship while navigating my "afters."

1

NEVER KICK A MAN WHEN HE'S DOWN

On July 4, 2001, I found out my parents were getting a divorce. How ironic—it was Independence Day. Things had gotten so bitter, so turbulent, that I had a feeling it was coming. I was 13 and my brother Brock was 7, and boy, were we in for a ride. I remember my mom telling me that both my parents loved us but they could no longer be together. I was okay with this because of how tense my relationship with my dad already was by then, and I think deep down I was looking forward to a life with him out of the house.

Finding out my parents were splitting up was the first of my forever moments. I would never be the same person as I was on July 3. None of us would be.

A few days after I was told about the divorce, my dad was diagnosed with testicular cancer and needed immediate surgery. This was a heavy time for me, finding out about the divorce and his cancer in one week. Within days, I found myself sitting in a waiting room at a hospital while my dad was in surgery.

"Mom, why are we here? You just told me you were leaving him."

My mom looked me right in the eyes. "Never kick a man when he's down."

This was a moment I will remember forever. I was dumbfounded. That sentence has stayed with me until this day.

Never kick a man when he's down? . . . Why not? I thought.

I was too young to appreciate how courageous and kindhearted this was of my mom. I knew she already hated him, but she stood by him through this, even though she couldn't wait to be away from him.

Loyalty, and sticking with someone through their worst of times, was a trait I'd later learn I inherited from her.

Although the divorce was looming, my dad stayed in the house for a bit while he recovered from his surgery. Talk about awkward. A few days after the surgery, I woke up to the sounds of my parents screaming at each other. Groggy, I stumbled downstairs and found them in the den a few feet apart, yelling, my mom's hands behind her back, holding something, but I couldn't tell what.

I could see the steam coming out of my dad's ears. Through clenched teeth he was roaring, "GIVE ME THE PHONE!"

Hmmm . . . What phone? I later learned my mom had kept a second phone hidden away in the house for emergencies, for the times when my dad would go crazy and lose his temper. This morning, my dad found the phone and, well, went crazy and lost his temper.

"*No!*" my mom stammered, taking a few steps back from him. Still her hands were behind her.

Sometimes my dad would get into these rages where he was unrecognizable.

All of sudden, he lunged at my mom and grabbed her. This happened *so* fast. I had never seen him get physical with her before. I don't remember anything other than my mom glancing at me—it felt like the look was full of shame, fear, embarrassment. Something switched inside of me and my heart ached for her. Then I lost it.

I shot up from the chair I had been sitting in and grabbed my dad, got him off my mom, and held him up against the wall by the collar of his shirt. My dad was over six feet tall and there I was, not even five feet tall on my tippy-toes, 13 years old, with a fist up to his face.

"If you ever touch my mom again, I will fucking kill you."

My mom was yelling, "HIL! GET OFF! STOP!"

I was *not* listening. She called the police and eventually separated us. I had totally forgotten my dad was just a few days out of surgery.

I stormed outside and tried to cool off. I sat on the curb and stared at the pavement, thinking over what had just happened. I couldn't believe how angry I had gotten, but I was so enraged seeing my dad try to hurt my mom. This was a scary moment, realizing for one of the first times that I had inherited my dad's temper.

A few minutes later, two police cars came driving down our cul-de-sac. The officers got out and approached me.

"Is he armed?"

"Armed? No, he's a coward," I said with 13-year-old attitude.

The cops went inside and tried to mediate the situation, but my family was already torn apart. They wrote up a police report, and that was it. I thought this would be the only time the cops were involved. Boy, was I wrong.

2

BEFORE THE CHAOS

Perhaps I should back up a bit. Before that chaotic week of my life, things were somewhat normal in my family. Although I don't remember too many good times shared between my parents, I do know that at one point they loved each other. I believe that in life, unless you have been caught in the rain, you cannot appreciate the sun, and without experiencing deep sadness, you can't have true happiness; and that is why I know that my parents could not have hated each other the way they did, without once having loved each other.

When I was six, Brock was born and I was excited to have a little brother. My dad was happy to have a son, and for a few years we would appear to be a picture-perfect family. We lived in the suburbs of Long Island, and from the outside, we looked like all the other families. My parents took us on a family vacation to Disney World, and I remember how normal everything seemed. This was the last time my mom and I were on a plane together, though, as we were never able to afford a vacation after that.

I don't remember too many positive times with my dad other than when he taught me how to tie my shoes. I often think back to that moment in his T-top convertible, as it's one of the few fatherly times I can hang on to. He was never an affectionate man. My grandma tells me that when I was a baby, he loved me and was a good father to me. I was his little princess back then. I don't remember those times, but it is reassuring to know he once cared for me like a dad should.

When my parents' relationship started to crumble, my dad's temper immediately became an issue. He would snap like a light switch. One minute he would be fine, and the next he'd be screaming through his teeth, his spit hitting my face, his pointer finger up next to my cheek.

As I got older, he constantly told me he would "put me on the streets" when I acted out, or that he would "bury me" when I stood up to him. I heard this so many times that if I got into trouble I would obnoxiously say, "Don't worry, Dad, I know you could bury me or put me out on the streets." An hour after his explosions he would act like everything was totally normal. His intense mood swings made it impossible for me to trust him. A lot of the time I felt confused; he was my dad—his one job was to provide for me, to protect me, but he constantly threatened to take that away from me.

My dad never physically abused us, but his threats affected me emotionally and mentally in ways I didn't realize until many years later. Because of the threats, I acted like a tough girl. I never backed down and always said what was on my mind. He would come after me and I would go toe-to-toe with him, stick my ground, always fighting back. He would yell; I would yell louder. I'd punch holes in the wall out of anger and frustration. My mom always made me spackle them up.

I remember most days coming home from school and walking into a Marlboro-smoke-filled house. My dad was always home, since he barely worked. Instead of throwing a baseball around or driving me to my friend's house, he would tell me he didn't have time to help me. I hated being alone in the house with him. I am proud of my 12-year-old little self, that I turned to writing in a diary as an outlet when I felt like I had nowhere else to go.

At night, I'd wake up to the sounds of his teeth grinding. I never understood how my mom could sleep through it. I would lie awake, staring at the ceiling. Always wondering why my friends' dads were so different from mine.

May 25, 2000:

    I came home from school and my dad was on the computer. The first thing he said to me when I walked in was "I can't take you anywhere. I have important work to do." I can understand that, but he didn't even say hi first. He sat back down at the computer while he was talking to me. He didn't even look at me. I called my mom to tell her I was going to hang out with my friends. I made a bowl of cereal first and then my tooth started bleeding. I went to tell my dad and he said, "Get out of here, I don't have time for this." I felt really unwanted. This is what I wanted to write before I get upset. Thanks for listening, kinda.

———

A few days after the police incident, both of my grandmothers came over to sit down with my parents in hopes of working everything out peacefully. My parents asked me to take my brother for a walk to give them some privacy. Brock and I walked around the neighborhood, and I tried to talk to him about what was going on, but let's be real—he was only seven.

When we got back to the house, both grandmas came storming out the front door, each of them yelling to us that it was the other parent's fault. Brock and I were confused. We thought they were there to help —not to be involved in the fighting.

My mom's mom came up to me and said, "Your father just said he is going to drag this out for as long as possible until your mother has nothing left." I stood and stared at her, not sure how to respond to something like that at 13. It turns out this was one of the few things my dad would ever keep his word on.

———

That summer, I was enrolled in a camp that traveled every week— either a few days out of state or day trips. Most of the girls at camp were from the North Shore of Long Island, which was generally a nicer, richer area than where I lived. I only enrolled in the camp because Jaclyn, my friend since I was 3 months old, convinced me to join.

A few days after my grandmas came over, I was at a baseball game with camp and while we were there, my counselor got a call from my mom saying she had to speak to me right away. The counselor handed me the phone.

"Honey, listen, the sheriff is coming today to get your dad out of the house because he will not leave. I just wanted to give you a heads-up that he won't be here when you get home."

"Um, okay. Thanks for letting me know."

Even though, per the divorce papers, my dad had to leave, he wouldn't. He felt that it was *his* house and his furniture since *his* mother had helped my parents when they'd bought the house. My dad's side of the family had money because they owned a few restaurants in New York City.

I went back to my seat and sat with my friends. Everyone was so happy. I thought it was unfair that I had to deal with this shit while everyone else had normal lives. My grandma always told me, "Don't air out your dirty laundry in public," so I chose not to speak to anyone about what was going on. I wanted to try to hide behind the image that I was a normal kid like they were.

The bus dropped me off at home later that day and I went to my front door, but my key wouldn't work. Annoyed, I started banging. Turns out my mom had all the locks changed out of fear my dad would come back. She told me that the sheriff had shown up, knocked on the door, and said to him, "You have 15 minutes to pack a bag and get out." That night was the first night without my dad in the house, and although it was weird, it was also weirdly peaceful.

A few weeks later, the police, lawyers, and my parents coordinated a day for my dad to come back to the house to pick up the rest of his things. When the day came, my aunt and uncle took Brock and me to the diner so we didn't have to be at the house during this ordeal. My uncle held my hand while he looked me in the eyes and told me, "No matter what happens between your parents, you will *always* have your uncle." I trusted him with every piece of me from that moment on. I always admired my uncle Rory because he had adopted my cousin after his dad walked out on him. I thought it was honorable that my uncle never had biological children but loved my cousin like his own. While my dad chose to have kids and did a shitty job, my uncle showed me that good fathers, and good men, do exist. My uncle was taken from this earth too soon, and I miss him deeply.

Rest in Peace, Uncle Rory
08/19/1957 - 11/27/2020

3

MOM, I GOT A JOB!

The following year, leading up to the summer, my mom told me that she couldn't pay for my summer camp that year. I was devastated, since camp had become an outlet where I didn't have to deal with my parents' drama. I had made such good friends and loved spending my summers traveling with Jaclyn. My mom said the divorce was too financially draining and camp was expensive. I asked my dad if he would pay, but he said no.

Throughout this book, when I refer to my grandma, I am speaking of my mom's mother. My dad's mother lost that title when she repeatedly helped my dad destroy my childhood.

I didn't know how I would be able to get back to camp, but I was determined to figure out a way. My grandma sat me down and told me she had a proposition for me.

"Honey, I'll make you a deal. If you get a job and start working, I will match whatever money you make, and hopefully by then you can afford to go to camp."

At first I thought this was total bullshit. None of my other friends had to work to pay for camp; we were only 14! But I had learned by that point that my journey was different, so I thanked her and said I would try to find a job.

I started browsing for jobs, but there was not much available for a 14-year-old other than babysitting, and that surely was not going to make me the money I needed to pay for camp. Child labor laws were also a problem because I needed to work more hours than the laws would allow. I felt defeated and was angry that money was controlling my life.

My aunt's ex-husband owned a catering hall/restaurant on a golf course, so I contacted him to see if he had any opportunities for me. Surprisingly, he told me he did! He set up an interview, and my mom drove me there and waited in the car.

About an hour later I came out smiling ear to ear.

"Mom! I got a job, and all you have to do is drive me there and back!"

"That's great, honey! I will definitely drive you. What kind of job?"

"Well, since I can't serve alcohol because I'm only 14, they're going to let me be the morning waitress for the golfers before the early tee time. My shift starts at 4 a.m."

My mom gaped at me, speechless, realizing she had just promised to be my chauffeur. Nevertheless, my warrior mom woke up every Saturday and Sunday morning for months and drove me to work at 3:30 in the morning. While most of my friends were spending their weekends sleeping late or at the beach, I was serving eggs and orange juice to golfers before the sun rose.

By the end of the spring, I had made enough money so that with my grandma matching it, I could pay for six weeks of camp. I was proud of what I had accomplished; this was the first time I earned something that I worked for. It would certainly not be the last.

When the time came to travel with camp, I was very nervous about leaving Brock home alone. I always protected him as best I could, but my parents were fighting so much that I didn't feel he was safe without me home. When my dad would come to pick Brock up, he would try to push his way into the house. Sometimes he'd call my mom 40 times a day harassing her, threatening her. Sometimes he would call just to have her pick up, and then he'd hang up. He would constantly tell my mom that he was taking Brock and never bringing him home. *What if something happens when I'm away?*

One day while my mom was at work, I came up with an idea I had seen in a movie. Brock and I picked a book from his (very advanced) bookshelf. We individually glued 100 pages together and cut a box out of the middle of the glued pages. I put a piece of paper in the cut-out box with my camp counselors' cell phone numbers and put the book back on the shelf.

"Brock, if anything happens and you need me, grab this book and go into the secret compartment, call one of these numbers, and someone will bring me the phone."

Why I didn't just put the piece of paper under his mattress or in a drawer, I don't know. At 14, this seemed more private and sneakier.

I am so thankful for my grandma and her promise. Working to pay for camp at 14 years old was one of the best lessons I have ever learned. My friends' parents gave them everything they wanted: designer clothes and bags, cars, family vacations, and weekly spending money. They never really appreciated any of it. Grandma's generosity taught me the value of hard work, and the extra pleasure you get from something you truly earned. This was a lesson I would never forget.

4

THERAPY, LEGAL GUARDIANS, AND CHILD PROTECTIVE SERVICES

Over the next few years, things between my parents got even worse. My mom did her best as a single parent to raise Brock and me, even though financially we were struggling beyond what most people knew. For a while, our groceries were being bought on my grandma's credit card. My mom didn't take any shit from us. If we didn't clean up after ourselves after a meal, we'd wake up in the morning with our dirty dishes piled in our bathroom sink. Brock was mowing the lawn by 13, and I had to do chores around the house. We did our own laundry as soon as we were old enough to work the machines. If our sports uniforms needed to be clean for a game, it was our responsibility to wash them. Mom made sure she raised strong, independent kids—and she did.

Several times over the years my mom had to go to court for restraining orders to protect her from my dad. He wasn't even allowed on our block unless he was there to pick up Brock or me. He would purposely do things to violate the orders and try to intimidate my mom, like drive into our cul-de-sac for no reason or park his car across the street to watch our house. Even when he was allowed there to pick us up, he wasn't permitted to step past our curb and had to keep his car on the street. Sometimes to be a dick he would pull into the driveway.

With a smirk on his face he'd say, "Well, this is *my* house, ya know?"

My dad argued that the furniture in the house was his, since he had owned it prior to my parents' meeting. The court agreed and he was allowed to take all of it. Our once-formal dining area with expensive chairs and a china cabinet was now empty—there wasn't even a rug. All that was left in the living room was a wall unit my parents had bought when they'd moved into the house. The rooms remained empty for a long time. It was hard walking into my house and seeing empty rooms, but my mom couldn't afford to buy furniture. My dad did not take these things for his own house. He didn't even have a house—he moved in with his mother. He put the furniture in a storage unit. All he wanted to do was hurt my mom, never once thinking about what he was doing to Brock or me.

When I was 15, Mom let me turn the garage into my "girl cave." She never kept her car in there since it was full of junk, things my dad hadn't taken and she didn't want on display. I made it my project to clear out enough space to hang with my friends. I bought myself a punching bag and would sit in the garage with Eminem and Linkin Park blasting so loud the entire block could hear. I would punch the bag for hours with the music blaring, trying to get out all my frustrations.

I always acted like a tough girl in my teens, but inside I was a marshmallow. I felt like I had to act tough since my dad always challenged me and I didn't want to seem weak—not to him, not to anyone. I always found myself sticking up for my friends in situations that didn't have anything to do with me, but I was protecting them just like I always protected Brock. Sometimes I'd get into fistfights. A few times I kicked ass; a few times I got my ass kicked. One night I came home with scratches, and my mom asked me what happened.

"I got into a fight, but don't worry—I didn't kick the girl when she was down," my smart-ass self said. I think I'd interpreted my mom's lesson from years earlier the wrong way.

My mom had a tape recorder attached to the house phone so anytime my dad called, she would have the conversation on tape to give to her lawyers in case he lost his temper and started threatening her, which happened often. This was super annoying for me as a kid because anytime I wanted to call my friends, I had to remember to turn off the recorder. This was in the early 2000s, before everyone had a cell phone. I would get so frustrated that this was what my life was like. I had some friends whose parents were divorced, but none of their situations sounded like mine.

Most of the times when my dad violated the restraining order or my parents got into an argument, the police were involved. Sometimes my neighbors would call, since my parents would be screaming at each other outside. Many times my mom would call. The cops never did much. When they would show up, my dad would turn on what little charm he had so my mom ended up looking like the crazy one. Over time, we got to know which cops would be sympathetic and which ones would just tell them to "try to get along."

———

One day during my junior year of high school, my guidance counselor, Chris Safina, came to my classroom door. Chris and I had a special relationship because I was often in his office talking about my parents. He was someone I could always talk to for advice on my family situation, and he was an important role model for me at the time. He was kind and compassionate, traits I wasn't used to seeing in a man. My good friend Andrew was in his office a lot with me too. Andrew was super smart but would skip class and hang in Chris's office instead. At our high school graduation, even though Andrew and I were only friends, Chris said to us, "You better invite me to the wedding."

This one day when Chris showed up at my class, he peered through the door window and motioned for me to come to the hallway. Excited to get out of class early, I jumped up and went. When I got to the hallway, Chris seemed more serious than normal. He looked at me and said, "Hil, I'm sorry to tell you this, but Child Protective Services is in my office waiting to speak to you."

"What? Why? What is Child Protective Services?" I asked, confused.

Chris explained that CPS got involved whenever there were domestic disturbances and minors were involved. Unsure of what they wanted from me, I hesitantly followed Chris to his office, where there were two people in suits waiting to greet me.

The CPS workers started rattling off questions. They wanted to know what had happened between my parents during their last fight—which, to me, was just another blowout argument. They wanted to know if Brock and I were getting physically abused and if I felt scared to be with either of my parents. They wanted to know more about the dynamics of my broken family. I was annoyed that these strangers were prying into my life. The police showed up often and never seemed to care much about what was happening, and now CPS suddenly cared about how Brock and I were doing?

"Never air out your dirty laundry in public" was what I was taught. This certainly felt like I was airing it out, and to strangers who could rip us apart, no less.

At the end of the meeting, the CPS workers casually told me they were heading to Brock's elementary school to talk to him.

"What?! What do you mean you're going to Brock's school?! He's only 10 years old!" I yelled helplessly.

I was enraged and sad. I was afraid that my brother would have to go through this alone. CPS told me this was protocol and they had to go. I was panicking, thinking about what my brother was about to go through, how confused he would be, and I wouldn't be there to help him. I also didn't want Brock to answer questions in a way that would make CPS remove him from the house. I started to cry.

This was not the last time CPS would be involved. Chris would show up at my classroom unexpectedly, and I knew CPS was there to talk to me about the most recent altercation between my parents. Nothing ever happened, except maybe a few reports got written and filed away somewhere. After a few rounds of this charade, Brock and I had handling the CPS workers down to a science. We knew what we had to say and how to respond to questions to get them off our backs unscathed.

———

As the divorce got more and more complicated, the courts assigned Brock and me a legal guardian. This person was supposed to represent us and speak for us at court, since we were minors. Sometimes I couldn't hang with my friends after school because I had to go "see my lawyer," which was obviously unusual to a group of teenagers.

For a while, my dad was fighting over custody of Brock. I was driving by now and my mom was working, so I'd have to take Brock to our legal guardian's office so he could talk to her about what he wanted. It was crazy to me that they would ask him questions about where he wanted to live—he was only 10! How could he really know what he wanted? How could they *think* he knew what he wanted? My dad and his mother would spoil Brock with the newest gaming systems, clothes, toys, whatever they could do to brainwash him that their family was better. My dad's mom would sit Brock and me down for dinner and say, "You know how horrible of a person your mom is, right? You should live here with us instead."

I was growing more and more resentful. Even though I didn't want to be with my dad, I thought it was really fucked up that he was not trying to get custody of me too. It hurt to think he didn't want me, even though I didn't want him.

One day my brother and I were sitting with our lawyer, and just as we were about to leave, she said, "You know, it's a shame. Your parents could have paid for Ivy League educations for both of you with the amount of money they've already spent on this divorce."

We didn't have furniture in the house, but they were spending money fighting over things they didn't have. They could have just sent us to Harvard.

———

Around this same time, my mom had me start speaking to a therapist, since it was obvious that I was becoming angry, erratic, and distant. I wasn't communicating well with my mom and always had a chip on my shoulder. Although I was reluctant at first, when I finally found a therapist I liked, he really helped me.

I'd speak to Dr. K. about what was going on with my parents, how alone I felt, how worried I was for Brock. I was terrified that I'd inherited my dad's temper and needed help controlling my anger. I had punched so many holes in the walls that I became a pro at spackling. Anytime I damaged the house, my mom made me learn how to fix it and do it myself. One time I ripped the refrigerator door off. That was a fucking nightmare to fix!

My therapist helped me get through these emotions and come to terms with things I wasn't ready to admit. He would always tell me that my issues stemmed from feeling "abandoned." I hated this word and didn't really feel abandoned, but Dr. K. drilled it into my head.

He was able to educate me on some of the reasons why my dad was acting the way he was. Dr. K. explained that my dad had manic episodes and was likely bipolar. My dad did not try to get help on his own, so he was never clinically diagnosed, but I am certain he struggles with serious mental health disorders.

At one point, Dr. K. suggested I go to a different therapist with my dad for group sessions. He thought it would be a conflict of interest if he worked with my dad and me together while also working with me alone, so he gave us a recommendation for another therapist. I spoke to my dad about it, and surprisingly, he agreed to go. I was *not* looking forward to this but felt trapped.

At the therapist's office, we sat on opposite ends of a long couch. The therapist asked us questions about our relationship, and I was brutally honest, which my dad didn't appreciate. I told her about the fights we got into; how he would threaten to bury me if I acted out; how he used money to bribe Brock and me; how his mother would talk badly about my mom, reminding us every time we saw her that our mom was "a horrible person." All these things caused me to act like a lunatic—I *hated* when they disrespected my mom, I hated that they wanted me to live in fear, I hated being around them, and suddenly, I was being honest about it.

Needless to say, this meeting did not go well. My dad and I started arguing, and before I knew it, he flew from his end of the couch toward me so we were nose to nose. He went full psycho-dad, yelling and screaming with a fist up to my face, flying spit and clenched teeth —what a surprise. I kept a straight face and stared at the therapist while thinking, *Told ya so!* I was almost pleased that he had finally shown this side of him in front of a professional.

When he finally calmed down, the therapist looked at us and said, "I'm sorry, but I don't think I will be able to help you."

I got up and left. I couldn't believe even a therapist was giving up on us. Talk about feeling "abandoned."

5

A DRUG-DEALING ENTREPRENEUR

As my parents' divorce dragged on, money problems got worse—way worse. My dad fought my mom over every little thing, legal bills were piling up, and my mom was struggling in a way that broke my heart. I was 17 years old now, so of course I needed some help from her financially, and even though I knew she wanted to help me, she never really could. I knew it made her feel shitty to have to say no to me all the time, so I needed to figure out a way to be in a position to not have to ask her.

My friends and I were good kids, but we drank and smoked weed like typical teenagers. One of my friends was selling weed, and I saw how much money he had. Then a lightbulb went off. *Why don't I do that?*

I was one of the popular kids in school and had a lot of friends. I figured I'd have a good network of people to sell to. I didn't know how to start my new business venture, but I spoke to a friend and he gave me a quarter ounce—7 grams—to sell. When I got the weed, I didn't even know how to open a baggie or how much each bag was supposed to weigh. I asked Andrew to come over to teach me the ropes. We were good friends, but I made any excuse to hang with him one-on-one, since deep down I cared for him as more than a friend.

Within a few days, I made a $40 profit. This was a lot of money to me, especially since it was a struggle to get my mom to give me $20 for the week.

Hmm, I can do this. I went back to my friend, who upped my stash and gave me a half ounce of weed—14 grams. Again, in a few days it was gone, I made more profit, *and* I was smoking for free—this was a double win.

A few weeks later I was at a friend's house and someone I hadn't met before was there. She introduced us and we made small talk. I'll call him Leo.

Leo caught on to the fact that I was selling weed and started asking me questions. He ultimately told me that if I was interested, he was a supplier and would give me a quarter pound of weed and I could have a few weeks to pay him back.

At the time, I had no idea how much that even was, but I told him I would think about it. We exchanged phone numbers and I left. I couldn't tell Leo I had only been selling weed for under a month, and only very small amounts at that.

I got into my car and looked up how much a quarter pound was. I almost passed out—a quarter pound was 112 grams. *HOLY SHIT!!*

This offer seemed too good to be true at first, but if Leo was willing to give me almost 10 times the amount I was getting, without me having to pay up front, I was definitely interested. I don't know why Leo offered to do this—probably just to impress my friend—but I honestly didn't care what the reason was.

Over the next few days I tried to figure out if I could even sell that much weed, since I was so new to this world. But if I could, it would make me more money than I had ever imagined, and I was *hungry* for money. So I devised a plan.

I knew I'd need help selling, so I turned to a guy I knew at school. I'll call him Jim. He was kind of a dirtbag, but we got along and I knew he sold weed too. He seemed trustworthy (at least for a dirtbag pot dealer). I found Jim and told him I had a proposition for him. I asked him if he would want to sell weed for me.

"What do you mean sell weed for *you?*" he asked, not knowing I had started my own little business.

I told him I would give him two ounces at a time and he would have one week to pay me back. My plan was to sell the other two ounces myself. Just like that, we had a deal. I thought in that moment I was the ultra-entrepreneur. Lowered my risk, raised my reward. I was *so* excited to get going and start making "real money."

A week or two later I met up with Leo, and he gave me the four ounces. This was *way* more weed than I had ever seen. I got home and put my head on it like it was a pillow. I was laughing so hard in my room by myself. *This is it! I am going to make all the money I need and won't have to bother my mom anymore!*

Within weeks, I was making hundreds of dollars. Between Jim and me, we were selling weed fast. Since we had different groups of friends, we were able to expand our customer base, and because the weed was good quality, people kept coming back for more. I felt like I was flying under the radar. I was a good student, never got into too much trouble, and no one suspected that a little Jewish girl from Long Island in honors and AP classes was selling weed.

One of my best friends, Julie, gave me the nickname "Haze-O-Hil," since I was selling so much. My girlfriends would ride around with me after school to do my afternoon drop-offs. They got a kick out of taking baggies to people all over town. I bribed the guy working at the local beer distributor to sell to my underage friends in exchange for weed. I would wrap up weed as presents for my friends' birthdays. I felt like a tough girl and was having the time of my life.

Suddenly, I had financial freedom. I was 17 years old, a senior in high school, and was able to buy whatever I wanted. Earlier that year I had bought my own car after years of saving money working at the golf course. Now I paid for my own gas, got tints and a sound system for the car. I bought my own clothes, went to the movies, and sometimes paid the entire bill when I went out to dinner with my friends. The best part was, I didn't have to ask my mom for anything. This was addicting. I really felt liberated with the financial burdens lifted.

Over the next few months Leo started giving me double my original supply. I was now picking up half pounds at a time. I had a whole system going, and it seemed bulletproof. Once he doubled my supply, my profits doubled, and I was even more hooked.

One day when I met up with Leo, he opened a shoebox and it was filled with pills. He told me they were Xanax and were his prime moneymaker. I had taken Xanax a few times with my friends but thought it was stupid, since you literally didn't remember anything the next day.

Leo told me he made most of his money off them, and once he told me *how much* money, my eyes widened as I stared at the pills.

I got quiet for a minute, contemplated an idea, and then matter-of-factly said, "I can get you Xanax."

At the start of my senior year of high school I had gotten a job working at a pharmacy. It was a small store, and two really nice guys ran the place. I helped them stock shelves, count pills to fill prescriptions, and do inventory.

I understand now that what I was about to do was one of the dumbest and most irresponsible decisions I have ever made.

I told Leo about my pharmacy job, which I had kept while I was selling weed because I knew my mom would get suspicious as to how I was making money if I were to quit. Leo told me if I could get him pills, he would trade me weed.

A few days later I got to work. I tried to act normal around my bosses, but inside I was shaking like a leaf. I knew I was about to commit a crime, but somehow I didn't care about the potential consequences. I waited until my bosses were both busy with customers and I snuck back to the controlled-substance aisle. The Xanax was kept in a drawer. I tried to be quiet, but my hands were shaking so bad the drawer started making noises. I started to cough, trying to cover up the creaks. I got the drawer open and saw an unopened bottle of 100 two-milligram Xanax. I snatched it and threw it in my bag.

This was the first time I stole pills from the pharmacy. I was *super* paranoid.

They definitely know what just happened. I looked around the store to see if anyone was looking at me. My heart was racing a million miles an hour. But no one was around. No one said anything to me. My bosses were acting totally normal.

Did I just get away with this?

I felt a surge of adrenaline that I was not used to, and I honestly hated it. Some people say they get a thrill off stealing. I certainly did *not* like the feeling. I was nervous and anxious, and felt very guilty. I didn't consider the legal consequences I could have gotten myself into or what was going to happen to the people who bought the Xanax. I felt bad that I was stealing, but honestly, all I was thinking about was the money I'd get.

The next day, I drove to Leo's house and he was excited to see the bottle of pills. Instead of having me pay him in full for my stock of weed, he deducted $400 from what I owed him and we traded. *Well, that was an easy $400....*

The next time I stole, I was just as nervous. Again, I waited for my opportunity to be alone and snuck back to the controlled-substance aisle. When I opened the drawer this time, I saw that the one-milligram Xanax came in bottles of 1,000 pills—10 times as many as the two-milligram dosage. This was a no-brainer for me. If I was going to steal, I might as well make the most of it. After I took this bottle, I became even more paranoid. Every time my bosses looked at me I thought, *Here it comes, they are finally going to confront me.* But they never did. Even though I was nervous, I was also becoming increasingly arrogant, since it seemed I was getting away with my scheme.

A few days later when I went to Leo's house, I showed him the bottle and he started to laugh.

"Holy shit, Hil! That's a lot of footballs!" he chuckled. *Footballs* was the nickname for one-milligram Xanax.

This turned out to be a financial game changer. Instead of making hundreds of dollars, now I was making thousands.

The concept was simple. Leo and I had a bartering system: 600 pills for four ounces of weed. By the time all was said and done, I had four ounces and the remaining 400 pills to sell, *all* for profit. Talk about the ultra-entrepreneur.

Part of me couldn't believe how many people in my town took

pills. Once I started selling them, I saw a whole different group of people than those who were buying weed. Parents would buy pills from me and make me promise not to tell their kids or my friends. Sometimes I would take advantage and offer them great "blueberry haze." They would always call me for more, telling me it was "the best weed around," when really it was just shitty weed with a few blueberry-flavored tobacco drops. Looking back, I feel like an asshole, but it does make me laugh that they fell for it.

Before I knew it, I had a drawer in my bedroom packed to the brim full of money. There were thousands and thousands of dollars in it that I had organized by denominations, all facing the same way. I put the serial numbers on the bills in numerical order—I was nuts. I'd never had money like that, and I was so happy that I didn't have to bother my mom. I always told myself if I made money and was successful, my first priority was to take care of her. A few times I brought home groceries with my "earnings." In reality, I knew how disappointed she would be if she found out what I was doing.

Finally, though, I was in control of *something*. My therapist always told me my parents' divorce was like a train accident: although I couldn't keep my eyes off it, I had zero control of the outcome and could only pick up the pieces after it was over. Although this seemed a bit intense and morbid, it was his way of explaining that I really could not control what was to come. But now, I *was* in control.

My grandma was paying for my cell phone at the time, and I felt it was wrong of me to be using that phone for my drug deals. I figured if I was going to be a drug dealer, I should at least be a respectful one! I bought myself a second phone and would buy prepaid minute cards at 7-Eleven so no one could track my calls. This would be my "drug-dealing phone." In the big picture, I was a small, small fish, but at the time, I thought I was fucking Scarface. When I would drive back and forth to Leo's house, which was about 20 minutes away, I would take apart my car door panel and stick the drugs in there like I was in a movie.

Over the course of a couple of months, I was making money hand over fist. At one point, I thought the owners of the pharmacy had started to catch on. I figured they had to have noticed that entire bottles of a controlled substance were going missing. Before they had the opportunity to confront me, I quit and used preparing for college as an excuse. I continued selling weed until I graduated, but my pill game was over—for now.

To reiterate: this was wrong, and I want to apologize to everyone and anyone who has been touched by drug abuse. I was feeding a drug problem that would run through my community for decades. Both Brock and I lost many friends and schoolmates to drug abuse, and addiction would smack me in the face a few years later. I was not only risking everything my mother and I had, but also my employers. They could have lost their business and their licenses, and I could have been prosecuted. At the time all I could see was money. Looking back, I see desperation.

6

SUNY ALBANY

As high school came to an end, I was looking forward to graduating and going off to college to get away from my parents' drama. My friends kept telling me I should write a book. They were seeing my parents' divorce playing out, and no one else was dealing with frequent police encounters, Child Protective Services, restraining orders, or therapists. My friend Cassie bought me a diary and wrote on the first page "pour your heart out and write your book! Love you!" My friends thought my life was crazy—and, thinking back, the craziness hadn't even started! Once they put the idea in my head, though, I knew I had to write a book and continue to document all my moments in my diary.

I applied to a few colleges but knew I wanted to go to SUNY Albany. I had to go to a state school because the tuition was cheaper, and when two of my cousins were at Albany I visited and loved it. When my acceptance letter came, it was an easy decision and I enrolled.

I majored in psychology because I was fascinated with how the mind works. This could have been because I struggled so much figuring out my dad. I was so intrigued as to why people did the things they did. I always wanted to help people, so I minored in criminal justice with the intention of eventually working with juvenile delinquents. I thought it was unfair that kids who got in trouble were immediately treated like criminals and bad people. I felt they just needed someone to talk to who treated them like a real person, and maybe that someone could help them turn their life around, instead of throwing the kid into the cycle of imprisonment and recidivism.

The reality was, the only difference between some juvenile delinquents and me was that I didn't get caught. If my bosses had ever found out that I'd stolen and sold Xanax, I would have faced serious charges. I didn't think I was a criminal or a bad person, so I knew that some other juvenile offenders weren't either. Their situations, like mine, caused them to do what they did. And all I had to deal with was a shitty divorce between my parents. I wanted to help others who needed a better shot.

I didn't know anyone else going to Albany. Through Facebook, which was brand new at the time and only geared towards college students, I found two girls who lived nearby and were enrolling, and I reached out to them. Marissa and Laura ended up being two of my best friends and eventually we lived together, but freshman year I was given a random roommate.

When I was matched up with my roommate, Sam, I thought we were going to hate each other. Sam lived on Long Island like me but had gone to private school. She was a cheerleader and homecoming queen with a nice family. I saw myself as a prior drug-dealing tough girl with a broken family and thought we would never get along. I was wrong. To this day, Sam is one of my closest friends, and these three girls eventually were bridesmaids at my wedding.

Always very social, I made a group of friends quickly. One night we partied in my dorm room. We got caught. Our resident assistant told us we had broken a school record: we'd only been at school for three days, classes hadn't even started, and we'd gotten caught with more alcohol than anyone ever had in a dorm. Instead of being kicked out of school, we were each given 100 hours of community service—that's what some convicted felons get! I felt like I was receiving the punishment I should have gotten for my drug dealing. We were put on academic probation and told we had to stay out of trouble.

Freshman year at Albany turned out to be one of the best years of my life. I got a job at the school gym swiping students' ID cards to allow them in. This was how I made my weekend spending money. My entire life, I *always* worked. I learned quickly, though, that I did not know how to study. High school had come easily to me, and I had passed my honors and advanced placement courses without having to put in that much effort. College was much different. One day while I was studying, a friend told me they took Adderall to get through the work. I asked for one, and when I took it, I felt like I had swallowed legal cocaine! I studied for eight hours straight and didn't eat anything. I passed my test with flying colors. I knew I needed more.

When my freshman year was over, I finished with a 2.7 GPA. My mom was disappointed and told me she was struggling to pay for my college and if I didn't get my shit together, I was on my own. I realized I could benefit from Adderall since I had done so well on the test I'd studied for when I'd tried it. I researched the symptoms of ADHD and called my primary care doctor on Long Island, who had been my pediatrician since I was three. I outlined all the "symptoms" I was suddenly experiencing. Easy as cake, I had an Adderall prescription before I knew it. I would take some and sell some, always finding a way to make extra money.

I was looking forward to a summer back home with my friends. I didn't know it, but it would turn out to be a life-changing few months.

7

JONNY

Going back home after being away at college for my first year was an adjustment. I had just found so much independence; I loved being on my own and not having to answer to anyone. A few weeks after all my friends got home from their colleges, our high school crew decided to throw a toga party.

The next chapter of my life was a direct result of what my friends and I went through on this night. Jonny was a friend of mine who was your stereotypical popular football player. He was incredibly handsome, kind, and funny and was the center of our group of friends. All the guys wanted to be like him and all the girls wanted to be with him. The night of the toga party was one of the best nights we'd ever have together, but it turned out to be one of the worst nights we'd ever have.

June 30, 2007:

A few nights ago was one of the hardest days of my life. The day started off great and turned into a nightmare. All of my friends are home from college, and we decided to throw a toga party. My girls and I went to the store and got things to make our costumes. We hung out all day, had a few drinks, and then headed to the party all dressed up. It was a typical party for us. The normal crew was there. We played drinking games, smoked, and laughed all night.

The boys were drawing tattoos on everyone. I got a cloud smoking a blunt, Julie got "Thug Life," Jonny got rosary beads with his football number, 20. We partied all night and I was happy when Andrew showed up. At the end of the night, Andrew, a few friends, and I hopped into Christine's car to smoke. We ended up stopping at a few people's houses and on the way to the gas station, we saw a major car accident. We couldn't tell who was involved or how many people were hurt. We just saw 10 to 15 cop cars, flashing lights, caution tape. We pulled over and asked someone on the street what happened and all they said was "He didn't make it." It was one or two in the morning, so we said, "Wow, that sucks, I guess we'll find out more tomorrow." We drove away like it was nothing.

I got dropped off later that night and turned my phone on silent, looking forward to sleeping late the next day since my mom and brother were leaving town. My brother is a genius and got accepted to a summer college course since he did a pre-test on the SATs and scored higher than most high school kids—he is only 13 years old! They left early and I was sound asleep. Around 10 a.m. I heard someone banging on my front door. I looked at my phone, groggy, and saw I had a ton of missed calls. I looked out my bedroom window and saw Julie's dad's car in the middle of my street. Then I heard Julie screaming, "HIL, OPEN THE DOOR!" I stumbled downstairs and opened the door. Julie was hysterically crying, her face soaked in tears, eyes bloodshot. I asked her what the fuck was going on. She took a deep breath and said, "Hil, Jonny got on his bike last night and he died."

I stared at her in silence.

"What? Who? JON? No, Julie, you are wrong. Jonny was just with us last night. He doesn't even have a motorcycle!"

"Hil, he's dead." Julie sobbed.

I didn't know what to do or how to react. I just started punching things. I ran upstairs and called my mom. I was hysterical. She picked up and said, "Morning, sweetheart!"

I started screaming, "MOM! JON DIED! JON IS DEAD."

She kept saying, "What? What are you talking about? What happened? I can't understand you!"

"Mom, Jonny got on a motorcycle after the party last night and he is dead."

"Oh, baby, I am so sorry. I will come home as soon as I get Brock settled."

I hung up the phone and kept punching things. Julie grabbed me and we hugged. I kept saying, "Julie, we were just with him, this can't be right."

Julie and I didn't know what to do at this particular moment—how could we? We were overcome with sadness and shock. We decided to call Jonny's two best friends to see how they were doing and try to get more information on what had happened to Jon. Both of them answered the phone so happy, thinking we wanted to make plans for the day. My heart sank as I realized they didn't know their best friend was dead. When we showed up at their houses, they knew something was very wrong as soon as they laid eyes on us. When we told them what had happened, we watched as our tough, strong guy friends dropped to their knees. Screaming, pleading, telling us we were wrong and this was some kind of mistake. The night before, we were all playing beer pong. Now we were driving door to door telling our friends that one of us was gone.

We started calling the rest of the group to tell them what had happened. We all decided to meet at Julie's house. Almost the whole group who was at the party the night before showed up at Julie's within minutes. We were all confused and panicked. Everyone was walking in circles, punching things, and kicking stop signs. Some of us were screaming at the sky. No one knew what to do. We had never experienced anything like this before. Not even 10 hours ago, we were all together, with Jon. And now he was dead? This didn't make any sense.

Eventually someone said, "Why don't we go to the site?" A bunch of us stopped, and the only thing that ran through my head was, "What site?"

We piled into cars and drove a few blocks, to the site where Jonny's accident was. The same site where I saw the accident the night prior. The same accident that we drove past and heard "the guy didn't make it"; the same accident we nonchalantly drove by saying, "Oh, we'll find out more tomorrow." We had no idea that it was our friend, our Jonny, dead in that accident. Jonny didn't even own a motorcycle, he was borrowing it from someone, so we had no clue it could have even been him. My entire body filled up with chills as I walked up to the site, making the connection and realizing that it was the place I had so casually driven by the night before. I was sick to my stomach. I felt so guilty, so disgusted with myself for not caring more the night before. I never would have thought it was my friend behind that caution tape. The accident must have happened minutes after we left the party, so we never even considered it was one of our friends. I will never drive past an accident again without thinking about the friends and family connected to the person who passed.

When we walked up to the site, we saw indents in a big cement wall, burnt oil on the pavement from the bike. We were all crying. Jonny's parents showed up and we all hugged and cried some more in a big circle. Seeing his parents made the pain so much worse. The accident site was in the middle of town, so people were starting to hear the news and see a crowd form. More and more people kept showing up. Eventually a priest arrived to say a few prayers. Here we were, standing around, with the ridiculous permanent marker tattoos still visible on our bodies. Crying, praying, screaming.

———

When a crowd started forming at the site, I saw Jon's ex-girlfriend, Jen. Jen and I did not like each other in high school, but when I saw her walk up to the accident site, I knew the drama between us was irrelevant. Jen was alone and clearly a wreck. I knew Jon and Jen had really loved each other, and I thought it was appropriate to put our bullshit to the side and be nice, knowing she was hurting too.

I walked away from my group of friends and went up to her.

"Hey, are you okay?"

She looked at me, surprised I had approached her. "No," she said with tears pouring out of her eyes.

"Neither am I."

Neither of us knew that would be the start of one of the most important relationships in both of our lives, for the rest of our lives. I think at the time we were just trying to be cordial and supportive. We exchanged numbers and I told her I would let her know when Jon's funeral arrangements were made.

———

The next morning I woke up early. I had spent most of the night tossing and turning thinking about Jonny and my friends. Losing someone in my group of friends, such a tight-knit group, really got to me. I had thought I was untouchable, that people like us didn't die in drunk-driving accidents. People were drinking and driving all the time. I know it's stupid, but it's true. We never expected someone to die. We were young and foolish. That morning I didn't know what to do with myself. Eventually I decided to go back to the accident site, to sit, to think, to pray, whatever that even meant.

Before I left my house, for a reason I still can't explain, I texted Jen instead of my friends. I told her I was going to the accident site, and she immediately got back to me that she would meet me there. About an hour later, we both showed up. The site was now full of flowers, balloons, pictures of Jon, and notes people had written to him. It had quickly turned into a beautiful memorial.

Practically strangers, Jen and I sat at the place where Jon had died not even two days earlier. We cried together, laughed together, lit candles. We shared stories about our memories with Jon. And as cliché as it sounds, we have been best friends ever since that day.

Growing up following my family's Jewish traditions, I had gone to Hebrew school, attended temple on holidays, and celebrated my Bat Mitzvah. But it never meant much to me, and I never really had a true belief in God. I think I was afraid to even let that thought into my mind, that something so far beyond my reach or understanding was controlling life's events. Like a lot of people, I felt that I did not have a reason to believe; nothing had ever happened to make me question, "How and why did that just occur?" And after all the shit I had gone through, if there was a God, why wasn't he helping my mom?

While we sat together, Jen told me what had happened to her the day she found out Jon had died. They had broken up about a year earlier, but she still loved him deeply. She always knew they would get back together again; she was planning on marrying him.

The last time Jen saw Jon was the day they broke up, and the last words she said to him were "Get out of my house—I hate you!" When she went to her bedroom after he left, she found a note from Jonny that said, "I am so sorry, Jen. I never meant to hurt you. I'll love you forever." She held on to that note, knowing in her heart that they would one day reconcile.

What happened to Jen the day she found out Jon died turned out to be a huge part of my story. She would eventually write a school paper about her life-changing moment, *her* Forever Haze of After moment, so I feel it is only right to share it in her words:

All I could think was that God was playing an evil trick on me. My chance was over, my time was up, and I was too late. Jon was gone forever. This was my fault, and I would have to deal with the guilt of being too late forever.

My legs suddenly felt weak and I collapsed to the ground. There was nothing left to do but pray. I put my hands together, looked up at the sky, and started helplessly screaming. This was the first time in my life I prayed with every single ounce of my body, my soul, and my heart. I was surrendering myself to the sky. It was the most real and unselfish prayer I ever said in my life. Every word I screamed came from the deepest depths of my soul. I cried to the sky, screaming that if it was really happening, if God was real and listening, and if it was really true that Jon was gone, all I could ask was that he was safe and in a better place. I begged God for a sign to let me know he was okay.

"Tell me he's with you, tell me he's in your hands," I screamed. "Promise me he's in heaven."

I didn't know how much time had passed, but I looked up and saw my friend standing in front of me. He had to carry me like a baby and put me into his car. I tried to speak over my heavy breathing, but all that would come out was loud, painful moans in between my sorrowful weeps. He told me I had to calm down or he wouldn't be able to drive the car. I started gagging and violently threw up out the car door. He put my seat belt on for me, reclined my seat, and told me to close my eyes until we got home. As we pulled away from the curb and up to the red light ahead of us, I lifted my pounding head. Through my hot tears I looked at the car directly in front of us. The license plate read "FAITH-L." I still couldn't speak, but I was saying the words "thank you" in my head, but that wasn't enough. I needed a bigger sign. We turned right. I could barely see out of my swollen eyes, and I desperately needed some fresh air. I hung my head out the window and looked up at the sky.

For a split second, all of my sadness and fears disappeared at what I saw. I was mesmerized by the most beautiful phenomenon I had ever seen in my life. I will never forget what it looked like. It was the most incredible sight my eyes had ever seen. Right above my head was a vivid perfect circle in the boldest and brightest colors of the rainbow surrounding the circumference of the sun. The lyrics to Jon's and my song now held their true meaning: Where do candy raindrops come from? A rainbow. I will forever thank Jon for mine.

That rainbow would change Jen's life. It would later change mine as well.

Jen got home that afternoon and couldn't believe the big, beautiful rainbow around the sun she had seen, seconds after she'd begged God for a sign. She couldn't sleep that night and googled "rainbow around the sun" to see if there was some kind of spiritual meaning behind it. Jen found text in the Bible that said a rainbow was a sign of the covenant between God and all the creatures of the earth. It represented forgiveness, and God's promise never to flood the earth again. God's promise that everything was okay, a symbol of hope, mercy, and love. For Jen, this clearly felt like a symbol of forgiveness between her and Jon, something they never got the chance to say to one another here on earth, but something that was definitely felt through seeing the beautiful phenomenon in the sky.

From this moment, Jen wholeheartedly believed that was her sign, that was Jonny telling her that everything was going to be okay and that he forgave her, as he knew from her painful prayers that she forgave him. Jen was able to accept Jonny's death in a different way than I could.

Over the next few weeks Jen and I were inseparable. I heard Jen's rainbow story so many times that I could practically recite it word for word, but every time she told me, I would sit and listen to every detail like it was the first time. The story was so compelling, so intense and spiritual, that even though I didn't really believe it, I still listened. I wished something like that would happen to me. I wished I could see something so perfect that I would understand and know that Jonny was telling me things were going to be okay.

Maybe I wasn't looking hard enough.

8

THE ARRANGEMENTS

Jen and I had only really known each other for a few days, but we both felt like we had been friends forever. There was a level of comfort between us. I knew Jen's heart was hurting like mine. We may have been grieving different kinds of losses, but we were grieving together.

The wake and funeral occurred a few days after Jonny's passing. His parents asked our group of friends to make picture collages to display at the wake. We sat around cutting up pictures while reminiscing, trying to prepare for the wake and funeral. A bunch of us had taken pictures with Jonny the night he died. Jon and I had taken one together, just the two of us, looking back over our shoulders showing off our newly drawn tattoos. It dawned on me that the night Jon died, he was dressed as a god in a toga, with rosary beads tattooed on him in permanent marker.

Jon's dad said he wanted one of our friends to write and read the eulogy. While all of us girls were together, my friends told me they wanted me to be the one.

I was hesitant and nervous at first. Then I realized this would be an opportunity for me to talk to Jon one last time. The process of writing the eulogy was strange. I had written in my diary for years and thought I was good at expressing my feelings, but writing something to my dead friend was, well, much different. I spent time in Jen's bedroom alone with just a pack of cigarettes to get me through. I struggled to write the eulogy, not exactly sure what to say to his parents and his little brother, who was in the same grade as my brother.

How do I tell these people that everything is going to be okay, when I don't even believe things are going to be okay? I paced around Jen's room trying to find the right words.

A few days later, my friends and I arrived at the wake together. We had never been through anything like this before. The knots in my stomach were uncomfortably painful. We got there early with Jon's family, and the funeral director asked my friends and me to wait in a separate room while Jon's parents and brother went in to see Jon for the first time.

We waited in silence.

Hearing Jon's mom scream and cry in agony the first time she saw her son in a casket was an experience that will be etched in my heart for the rest of my life. My friends and I heard her clearly from the room next door, and we all broke down. We were all hurting so badly, but his mom's scream—that was something beyond our understanding. That pain was so raw, we felt it through our bones.

When we were allowed into the room, we walked in cautiously and slowly. Seeing Jonny in a casket was surreal. In the Jewish religion, caskets are always closed. I had never seen a dead person before. It was horrible to see my friend lying there. Somehow, he still looked so handsome. We all silently gazed at the casket, in disbelief that this was Jon, who we were just partying and laughing with a few days ago. It was such an eerie and disorienting feeling.

When the funeral home opened its doors, hundreds of people waited in a long line to pay their respects. Shortly after, I was called up to deliver the eulogy. My girlfriends and Jen stood shoulder to shoulder with me for support. I was speaking for all of us. There were so many people who came to the wake, they set up speakers in the parking lot for the people waiting outside. Nervous but determined, I read Jon's eulogy. Only 19 years old, standing two feet from Jon's open casket, I spoke to my friend:

When I heard my girlfriends nominated me to do the speaking on behalf of Jon, it was a bittersweet feeling. I have so much to say, so much I would like to still say to Jon, to his family, to his brother, and to my friends. First and foremost, I would like to thank his parents for raising such a great kid. I don't know if you truly understand how many genuine, positive characteristics you passed down to Jon, but I think I speak for our entire group of friends when I tell you that you truly raised one of the best. To his brother, Cammy, there is nothing I can say to take away any bit of the pain you are feeling, however I would like to stress to you that you are not the only one going through all the emotions that you are feeling, and I hope you know that any one of us will be there for you for the rest of your life, to cry with and to laugh with. And although you never had a sister, you now have me, and the rest of my girls, who are gladly taking you under our wing and will do our best with the boys to guide you through life and help you over every obstacle, just like Jonny would have done, and just like Jonny would like us to do.

For those who really knew Jon, everyone knew he was a gentle giant. Everyone knew that Jonny had the biggest heart and the smallest bladder. There is not one negative quality that comes to my mind when I think of Jon and the life he lived. For his family, everyone knew how much of a compassionate, genuine person he was. For any past girls he was involved with, they knew how much of a love he was. For any past people that tried to get in his way, they knew how strong and dedicated of a person he was. And for his friends, we saw all of those qualities; how much of a selfless, loving, dedicated person he was. Every one of us knew that no matter what time, what situation, or what the reason was, if we ever needed anything, Jonny would be the first person there by our side.

I was one of the lucky people to have spent the last seven years of Jonny's life with him. Seventh grade was when I met Jon, and from that point on we were good friends ever since. Almost any funny story I tell, Jon's name pops up. Like when he fell asleep on my dog's bed and got up and was covered in dog hair… Or when in senior year in the middle of a class we had together he interrupted the class to crack a joke on our Jewish teacher and said, "What is Mr. Stein in a hot tub?" and the whole class stared at him and he responded, "Matzo-ball soup." Jon was a complete and total character, and he did anything in his power to make sure that everyone around him had a smile on their face at all times, and we always did.

I'm going to miss the constant smile on his face, the times we all hung out in his backyard, the many afternoons we spent at his house before basketball games senior year, the way he laughed, the way he communicated with people... And the way he told you to pick him up in 10 minutes, and 45 minutes later he would peek his head out the door while he was in a towel and would tell you he would only be 1 more minute, and that's when you knew you really only had 15 more minutes to wait. What I would do to just wait one more time. The things I would do.

I know Jonny is listening now. I know he hears everything I say and I know he will be there with the rest of us forever, and just like he was always there for us when he was around, I know he will continue to be there for us, because his soul did not die along with his body. I hope that we all learned a strong lesson from this terrible tragedy. I send my deepest, deepest condolences to his family, but I hope you all see how much Jon really meant to every life he touched. Cammy, I hope you can eventually move on with your life and not necessarily live up to be just like your brother, because you don't have to, but maybe grow up and try to fulfill any dreams your brother did not have the time to do. And if Jon's dreams are not the same as yours, then I hope you can take the same stance as Jon did when he strived to accomplish something, with the pride, integrity, and determination he held in his hand.

Life has a strange way of working out, and deep in my heart I know that if Jon was given the chance to continue his life, he would have been one of the greatest football players. But things don't always work out as planned, and maybe there was a reason that Jon's life had to end so soon, but I will say that Jonny lived a full life in the years that he was around for. They tell me everything happens for a reason, so I am waiting to figure out the reason why they had to take him, why one of my best guy friends, why an amazing son, why a great brother, why a best friend to so many of my close guy friends. Our core group of friends will never be the same, and we have all accepted and understood that. It is horrible that something so tragic and so sudden had to happen to bring us closer *together, but I believe that maybe this was the reason. Maybe all of us needed each other this much throughout all our friendships and it just took this to realize that. From now on, whenever any of us hear of a similar terrible tragedy, instead of just changing the channel or flipping the page in a newspaper, I think all of us will send our thoughts and prayers to the family and friends of the person who was involved in it.*

I spent Jonny's last night with him, and I find it quite ironic that in the past two years I never brought out my camera, yet that night something made me grab it. Me and Jon took a bunch of pictures and all Jonny kept saying to me was "Tonight we are capturing every moment, Hil," and so we did. Although Jon's body is gone, his spirit and soul will live with me and every other life he touched forever.

To Jonny, I wish I could just call you one more time, hang out with you once more on Tommy's boat, have you sitting in my front seat just once more controlling the radio and forcing me to listen to Backstreet Boys. Just once more I want a Jonny hug, just once more I want to see you walk through my backyard. . . . I have realized all of this is impossible, so, babe, you have a lot of us waiting to see you, so please save us a bunch of seats. I miss you more and more as each day passes by, and until you open up the gate for me, I hope that you stay by me and help me through whatever comes my way. You will remain in my heart forever, and there is not one day that is going to pass by where the first thing I think about in the morning isn't your gorgeous smile. Keep smiling on us.

You truly are God's most handsome angel.

Love always, Hil

Before I walked away, I folded up the eulogy and put it in Jonny's suit pocket so it could be buried with him. I gave him a kiss on the forehead and cried. *Rest in peace, my friend.*

Rest in Peace, Jonny
03/09/1988–06/24/2007

———

The next day was the funeral. My friends and I woke up early and tried to prepare ourselves for the day ahead. Our parents arranged for a limo to drive us to the church and cemetery, since they knew we would not be okay. Showing up to the church was dreamlike. We were all dressed in black, unable to control our tears and overcome with emotion.

The church was filled over capacity, with people standing, lining the outer rows. It was bittersweet to see how many people Jon had touched, how many people wanted to be there for him.

We listened to the priest talk about the suddenness of Jon's death and how he was in a better place with God now. I would be lying if I said I agreed with this. At the time I was still angry at God, thinking, *How could you do this? Why would you take him, now?* It didn't make sense to me that Jon was in a better place. I felt that here, in real life, was better.

When the funeral started, my guy friends were the pallbearers, and they stoically carried Jon's casket on their shoulders. It crushed me to watch them trying to be so strong, knowing they were broken inside.

We arrived at the cemetery and gathered around Jon's parents and brother, trying to be strong for them. Next to Jonny's plot was a headstone for a four-year-old girl. None of us knew who this little girl was or how she had died, but we felt a weird comfort thinking Jonny would be watching over her, and I am confident that he is.

The priest started his sermon and said that in his whole career, he had never seen so many people at a burial service. My friends and I huddled around together, staring at the casket, still in disbelief that this was happening. As the casket was lowered into the ground, a lot of us dropped to our knees as the weight of the situation took us down. We were hysterical, beginning to accept the fact that this was real.

After the funeral we went back to Jon's parents' house, which became our "hang out" spot for the remainder of the summer. His parents filled the house with pictures of Jonny, his football picture enlarged in the center of the living room. We tried our best to support his family, even though there was nothing anyone could do to minimize the pain.

We walked into Jon's room, solemnly looking around, touching and smelling his clothes. We laughed when we found a speeding ticket he got Jet Skiing the week before. Then we cried, instantly remembering that he was alive and having fun just a few days ago. And now, he was gone.

9

"EVERYBODY DIES"

As the summer continued, Jen and I spent almost every day together. We were going through a spiritual journey that we couldn't understand at the time, but we were going through it together. Jen and I would talk about Jon tirelessly. Jen would tell me what it was like when they were dating, how much they both loved each other, and how they would plan and dream about their future together.

Jen would relive her rainbow moment and I would sit and listen, over and over again. Even though I hadn't seen a rainbow, I was starting to believe that what had happened to Jen was a real sign. Jen was sure the rainbow was from Jon, that he sent it to her moments after she found out he was gone and begged for a sign from God. One day Jen woke up crying and couldn't control her sadness. Losing Jon was unbearable to her; the pain of never being able to speak to the love of her life again was too hard to accept. She ran an errand later that day, and her tears continued. She pulled into a parking lot and broke down in hysterics, her head buried in the steering wheel. When she looked up, the car in front of her had a license plate that read "MY-RAINBO."

It was getting harder for me to believe the sign wasn't real.

———

Before I went back to college, my dad told me he wanted to see me. I had told Jen a little about him and our relationship, but it's hard to understand until you see it.

Jen's dad was affectionate, loving, sympathetic, and spiritual. He actually called Jen the day Jonny died to tell her about this "unbelievable rainbow around the sun" he'd seen, without knowing that that same rainbow had changed Jen's life and without knowing Jon had died. The second he heard the news, he sped over to Jen's mom's house to be there for his daughter, to hug her and give her a shoulder to cry on.

Jen has two younger brothers; they all have different moms but the same dad. At Christmas, all three moms will be sitting together at a table—everyone gets along. At first I thought this was very strange. Then I realized that they were actually the normal ones, being able to coexist and not separate the kids on holidays for selfish reasons. I already knew my family dynamic was different—but Jen's situation reinforced that for me, since my parents couldn't even be on the same block as each other. I loved being around her family, because it was so beautiful and different from what I was used to.

Jen told me she would come with me to see my dad so she could meet him. I told her I didn't think it was a good idea, but she insisted.

I finally agreed. "Okay, Jen, I warned you."

We showed up at my dad's mother's house and he was standing in the garage. As we were walking up the driveway, he immediately started giving me a hard time about how I hadn't seen him much that summer, even though he knew Jon had passed away the month before.

"Dad, give me a break, I've been a little preoccupied this summer. . . ."

Without even looking at me, he said, "Hil, I don't know what you're so upset about—everybody dies."

His coldness stopped me in my tracks. I felt like I'd been punched in the stomach. I looked at Jen and her eyes filled with tears. I looked back at my dad.

"Wow, Dad. A fucking hug would have been nice."

This was the sad reality of how he was. Another reminder of how I never felt real love or comfort from him. I can't remember the last time my dad hugged me or showed me any kind of affection. Jen was startled by his statement. My dad was so emotionless and unfeeling. Everybody does die, that's true, but that was not what I needed to hear at that moment. I looked at Jen and whispered, "I'm sorry."

We sat through a dreadful dinner and left as quickly as possible. We got into my car and Jen turned to me.

"Hil, you were right. I didn't understand what you meant about your dad until right now. Now I understand, and I am so, so sorry. Please know you are nothing like him. You are *nothing* like him."

———

As that terrible summer came to an end, I packed up to go back to college. In my heart, I felt that I was a different person after my spiritual summer. When I entered college my freshman year, I tried to maintain my tough-girl persona from high school, but after Jon died, that wasn't important to me anymore. Now I wanted to be honest and kind—not angry and tough. All my college friends knew what had happened and would listen to my stories about Jon, Jen, and her rainbow. When our friends would see a rainbow, they would send us a text, reminding us that the story had touched them and they believed. One of my best college friends, Amanda, would sit with me outside the library and we'd talk about faith and spirituality for hours. We'd sit with our iced coffees and cry and laugh together over Jon and people she had lost. It was therapeutic for me to have friends at college I could talk to about what was going on back home.

Jen came up for her first visit to Albany about a month into the semester. We woke up hungover on Saturday and decided to go to the diner. Over the entire course of breakfast, we talked about Jon, and without sparing any detail, Jen again told me her rainbow story. She was so sure Jonny had sent her the rainbow to prove he was okay and that he was still around. I knew I had a choice. I could either choose to believe or choose not to. I wanted to believe.

"I just wish I could see something for myself. I wish I had my own sign," I looked at Jen and said.

Sitting across from me at the table, Jen wished that something would happen to me too, so I could believe it for myself. We finished breakfast and headed back to campus.

On the ride back to my dorm, we stopped at a traffic light and Jen caught a glimpse of something to her right. She noticed people in the car next to us with their phones out the window snapping pictures. Once again, she couldn't believe her eyes. Jen was shrieking, "HIL! PULL OVER—PULL OVER RIGHT NOW!"

From one side of the world to the other, there was a big, bright, beautiful rainbow that looked like it touched both ends of the earth. You could see every color so clearly, it looked like someone had painted the rainbow in the sky.

Jen was screaming, "OH MY GOD! THERE'S A RAINBOW! HIL! YOU ASKED FOR IT AND YOU GOT IT!"

I pulled over to the side of the road. Jen was freaking out, but I was speechless and couldn't say anything. Jen could not understand how I wasn't reacting the way she was. She kept saying, "Hil, you just asked for your sign! Here it is! How are you not freaking out right now?"

I was trying to comprehend that the rainbow was actually there, moments after I had asked for my sign—there it was. Just like Jen had asked for her sign and gotten it, now I got mine. I honestly could not believe it. If it weren't for the other people on the road taking pictures, I would have thought I was hallucinating.

There wasn't any rain that day and there wasn't a cloud in the sky. There was no Mother Nature–like reason for a rainbow to be there. It was seemingly "random," but not random to me.

I turned to Jen with tears in my eyes and said, "Thank you."

I finally felt like I had a rainbow, for me.

10

MY FOREVER HAZE OF: FAITH

After these few months, my life had been forever changed. Jonny and I were not best friends, but losing someone in your core group of friends like that, so suddenly, had a way of shaking up your life. I was affected spiritually, emotionally, and mentally.

I now fully believed we could die at any moment. I had never felt that before; I never really thought about death at 19 years old. After Jon died, it became something so scary and real. We were all together one minute, and then a few minutes later, Jon was gone. The suddenness of the situation was shockingly terrifying to me.

After that night, I understood how short life is. I wanted to be a better person because of it. I wanted to listen more carefully, I wanted to care more deeply, I wanted to love harder.

I took Jon's death as a lesson to help me with my parents. I spent a few days writing each of them a letter, pouring my heart out to them. I begged them to stop fighting. I pleaded with them that life was too short. I told my mom I wasn't trying to hurt her by trying to maintain a relationship with my dad; I was doing it so I knew in *my* heart that at least I had tried. I kept thinking, *If I or my dad dies tomorrow, I want to know at least I tried.*

I begged my dad to stop being so hateful and conniving toward my mom. I tried to reason with them that neither of them had a pot to piss in, but they were fighting over money that didn't exist. I told them they had to let go of the hatred in their hearts, that life was too short to spend it with this much negativity.

Maybe I was naïve in thinking that my experience could somehow change the course my parents were on. It ultimately did not change anything, and neither of them changed their behavior. What I was going through was my own journey, not theirs. If it weren't for Jon, though, I would never have written to them. I would never have at least tried to convince them to change. So, for that, I am thankful that Jon inspired me to do so.

I also changed in the sense that I now had hope in what I refer to as "blind faith." This was not a religious belief; it was just something I felt in my heart. I did not think there was a God sitting on top of a cloud controlling every minute of every person's life, but I did believe that things that were transpiring were not just coincidences. I did not believe the rainbows were random events. I believed that things were happening and they were happening for reasons outside of my understanding, but that was okay. I felt a sense of spirituality and connectedness that I had never felt before. I opened my life up to the possibility that people who died could truly contact you in ways that could be uncomfortable but also beautiful.

I think by allowing myself to believe, I opened myself up to be a receiver. Things that hadn't happened yet might not have happened if I hadn't given myself the opportunity to believe.

I had entered my Forever Haze of After, and I was never the same person as I was the day before Jon died.

11

"BE NOT AFRAID"

My college roommates and I decided we wanted to get a house off campus for our junior year. My college friends and I were so close, they were like my family. Most of them knew I wanted to write a book and supported me in doing so. Our group had eight boys and eight girls; we partied hard and studied harder. We'd make a concoction called "Skippy," which consisted of a 30-pack of cheap beer, a handle of cheap vodka, and lemonade powder mixed up. Somehow, we thought it was delicious, although now the thought of it makes me want to throw up. The morning after a party, we'd wake up and be banging at each other's doors to go to the library.

My girlfriends and I looked into our housing options at the beginning of sophomore year and were so excited to make it our reality. When I called my mom and spoke to her about it, she told me there was no way she could afford off-campus housing. My dad had dragged the divorce out so much that she was relying on my room-and-board discount for single parents, which was how she was paying for me to be at school in the first place. Once again, money controlled my life.

As I struggled to figure out what to do, I saw my friends happily call their parents and get the okay to proceed with the house. I was jealous that this was so easy for them. I came home for winter break sophomore year and told my friends I was going to try to figure something out. Here I was, again with no financial help, trying to find a solution on my own.

January 14, 2008:

If I think about the best decision for the future, it is definitely for me to take a semester off and work full-time to save money for junior year. I'm sad because this is the last thing I thought would ever happen. I just know that I can't depend on my parents for money or help. I can be upset that I won't be at my escape home in Albany with my best friends for a semester, or I can take this as what it is, grow up, work, and take night classes while I am home. I came into Albany with nine AP credits, so if I take two classes while I am home, I won't fall behind academically when I reenroll. I am going to take control of the situation. I am going to do whatever I have to do to get this house, and fuck everybody else.

I spoke to my mom about my idea, and she told me that if that was what I wanted to do, she would support me as long as I took some courses from a local college to stay on track academically. I spent a few days calling Albany to figure out the process, and within days, I had withdrawn from college and enrolled in night classes at a local community school.

I texted my roommates and told them I had to talk to them. We all lived on Long Island, so we met at a pizza place and grabbed dinner. While we were eating, I told them that I had withdrawn from Albany for a semester and explained to them my plan.

Everyone dropped their forks and stopped eating. They looked at me shocked.

"Hil, are you *really* going to come back?" they asked.

I was equally shocked by their question. "Of course I'm going to come back! That is the whole reason *why* I'm leaving!" I assured them.

My friends later told me that no one believed that I would be back. Most people who withdrew stayed home and continued working and never finished college. That was *never* my plan. Jen took the drive with me to Albany to empty out my dorm room. It was an emotional ride for me. As much as I knew there was a purpose for what I was doing, I was angry and sad that I had to be doing it in the first place. I felt resentment toward my parents, feeling like if they had just acted differently, my life could have been different.

Just like my legal guardian had told me, they could have paid for Ivy League educations for Brock and me if they had stopped spending so much money fighting through the divorce. Now, they couldn't even help me with a $500-a-month house payment.

Within a week of being home, I found a job through a temp agency where I would be working as a receptionist. The lesson I'd learned when I was 14 when my grandma helped me pay for camp was in the back of my head the whole time: work for what you want and earn it. I worked from 9 a.m. to 5 p.m. and then twice a week drove straight to a community college, where I took classes until 9 p.m.

Once again, I had to earn and work for what I wanted. And so I did.

———

Once I was home and settled, I started to see Dr. K. again. He helped me deal with my feelings about Jonny, my anger about being home, and my dreams. Some dreams were about Jon; he'd be with my friends and me, hanging out. They felt *so* real, like I was really speaking to him. In one of them I thanked him for my rainbow, and he said, "I'm glad you knew it was from me."

I went through a period where my dreams were weirdly coming true. I went to see a psychic since I was starting to get freaked out, and as soon as I sat down, she asked me if I was clairvoyant or had "visions." I would dream about a person I hadn't seen in years, and the next day I'd run into them—this happened *numerous* times. I'd dream about my dad after not speaking to him for weeks, and the next day he'd call. I always knew when I would hear from him thanks to my dreams. I appreciated the warnings, but it was getting creepy.

In high school, I had a friend who got himself into a bind and asked me if I could spot him some weed so he could "get back on his feet." Without hesitation, I lent him more than $2,000 worth of weed and pills. I never heard from him again. He lived in a different town, so we never ran into each other. He had been a close friend of mine, and I felt incredibly betrayed and angry that he had stolen from me. Loyalty and companionship were always important to me, so I couldn't believe what he had done. I held this grudge so hard that I would constantly think about what I would do to him if I ever saw him again. I was being somewhat hypocritical, since after Jonny passed away I tried to let go of all my grudges, but this one hurt my ego and I couldn't get past it.

One night I had a dream that I shot and killed this friend. It was terrifying and made me feel out of control and dangerous. I saw him dead in my dream, and it was my fault. A few days later I received a phone call that he had overdosed and died. The next time I saw him was at his funeral, and I had an overwhelming sense of guilt that I had wished such bad things on him, and now he was gone. While I stared at him in his open casket, chills filled every inch of my body as I realized I had seen him dead, just like that, in my dream a few days earlier.

The issue with some of my dreams coming true was that, of course, some did not. I had a dream once that Jen and I got into a horrible car accident. For weeks I was super anxious anytime we got into a car together, thinking it was just a matter of time until we were going to be dead on the side of the road. I was anxious every time I woke up from a night full of vivid dreams—really, really anxious.

During a session with my therapist, I was explaining to him that I was living in fear over my dreams. He then asked me, "Do you know what one of the most repeated commandments is?"

"Ummm, thou shalt not kill?"

"No—it is 'Be not afraid.' "

I looked at him weirdly, letting the words sink in. *Be not afraid.* I liked that. He told me I shouldn't be afraid of my dreams, regardless if they were metaphors or hints of the future. He said I had to just live and look at my dreams as warnings and insights. *I would love the Lotto numbers, dream gods!*

I got home that day and thought about my therapy session, the words *be not afraid* repeating in my mind. I couldn't stop telling myself to "be not afraid." Not of my dreams, not of my dad. Within a few days, I did what any other 20-year-old does when they find a phrase they like—I got it tattooed on my foot.

The words *Be Not Afraid*, surrounded by angel wings, the wings filled with the colors of the rainbow.

12

"YOU MAY NOT ALWAYS HAVE MONEY, BUT YOU'LL ALWAYS HAVE YOUR RAINBOWS"

February 12, 2008:

Losing somebody you love is definitely the greatest pain I think someone could ever feel. I started a new job a few days ago, and one of the guys that work there is named Johnny. The job is fine. I go in to work every day knowing I am one day closer to Albany, to living in my own house with my girls. My friends and I hung out at Jon's parents' house for Super Bowl, and it was emotional. Every time we are there it is a reminder that he isn't there.

My dreams have been crazy lately. A lot of weird shit is happening and coming true. I had a dream that Jen was mad at me because I wouldn't get her mozzarella sticks. The next day I went to her house and she said, "Let's get mozzarella sticks with dinner"—what the hell?! I had a dream my cousin broke up with his girlfriend. I spoke to my grandma the next day, and she told me they split up. I haven't spoken to my dad in weeks, had a dream about him—the next day he called. Weird.

Call me crazy, but I believe at Jonny's wake he heard my eulogy and I think he appreciated it and maybe that is why he comes through to me in my dreams. I hope he continues to visit me.

A few days later, I was sitting at work and received a Facebook notification that I had a private message. I saw that it was a girl from high school, but we weren't really friends, so I figured it was sent to me by accident. I logged on to my account and started to read:

February 18, 2008: Hey Hil, I just thought I'd tell you . . . For the past two nights I've had the same dream about Jonny, and it's not just like a dream with him in it. It is a dream, but it's him telling me to tell "Hil's crew" that he's chillin' and wants me to tell you guys that he's gotten his wings. The first night I had the dream it just kinda felt like a dream, but when I woke up this morning it really felt like he was mad that I haven't already told you. This may seem totally weird to you and if it does I'm sorry but I don't want to piss him off any more haha. So, he's chillin' and he has his wings. I'm sorry if this is too weird.

Goosebumps covered every inch of my body. The last diary entry I wrote, on February 12, I said I hoped that Jonny would continue to visit me in my dreams. Six days later, someone writes me out of the blue to tell me Jonny visited her in *her* dreams to relay a message to "Hil's crew" that he had gotten his wings?!

I read her message a few times. I wondered, *Jonny, why didn't you just come and tell me directly?* But then I realized, maybe he wanted to spread his presence so more people could believe he was still around. I sent the message to my friends, to relay the news that Jonny had sent us. Some believed it, some didn't.

I chose to believe. It was getting harder for me to believe that he *wasn't* around.

———

March 23, 2008:

It's Brock's 14th birthday today! Crazy how my little brother is growing up. I wonder all the time what we are going to end up like when this divorce is over, especially Brock, since he's so young. Last week my parents went to court and my dad got the court to agree to lessen his child support. The divorce agreement says if a child is working full-time, child support ends. So, my dad decided to argue that I was home working full-time and he didn't have to pay for me anymore. The whole reason why I am home working full-time is because they won't pay for my college! How the fuck could the courts agree to this? I was pissed, so I called my dad yelling and he told me that instead of giving my mom the money every week, he was putting it into a bank account for me to have when I get back to college. YEAH, RIGHT is he going to do that. My mom told me that things are going to get tighter and now she needs my help with the bills since I am home and living in the house. So now, some of the money I am earning to get BACK TO COLLEGE is really going to my mom to help pay bills. . . . Meanwhile the whole reason why I am home is to pay for my OWN college, not the electricity bill! When I bitch at my dad, he tells me he can't believe that I am complaining since the money will ultimately be mine. Of course, I don't believe him.

When the courts agreed to suspend my child support, I felt like I was being punished for trying to be a responsible adult. The courts did not care *why* I was home working; they read the agreement and backed up my dad—end of story. Spoiler alert: When I got back to college, there was no bank account waiting for me. I didn't get any of the money my dad told me he was saving for me. The one thing I could always count on him for was empty promises.

My dad never thought anything he did was wrong. Not when he took the furniture out of the house and put it in a storage unit, not when he stopped paying child support, not when he would threaten us —never. It was only during random moments of reflection he had that he would send us cryptic text messages apologizing for everything he'd done in one sweeping, semi-heartfelt statement. And even during those times, he never really took ownership of what he put us through.

———

March 27, 2008:

I told my mom I had to go to the dermatologist and I was making an appointment. I called and they told me I couldn't make an appointment since money was owed on my account—surprise, surprise. Then I decided to check my Albany account and there is a hold on it, since I still owe money from last semester—shocker! I went to the dentist a few days ago, and the receptionist told me my insurance company had dropped me. Surprised? Not at all! I got home and opened a fortune cookie and it said, "All the news you receive will be positive and uplifting"—HAHAHAHAHA. I laughed so hard and read it to my mom. She laughed and said, "There's always tomorrow, right?" I looked at her and said, "No, Mom, Jonny taught me, there is not always tomorrow."

———

April 8, 2008:

I am going to be 20 tomorrow! I'm happy since I need a day to look forward to. Yesterday I came home from work and when I walked into the bathroom the light didn't turn on. Then I realized none of the lights were on in the house. I found a Post-it note from my mom that said we owe over $1,500 and our electricity was turned off. Couldn't go on my computer, couldn't watch TV, couldn't do laundry. I decided to go to the gym, went to the fridge—no water came out. Shit sucked. I sat on the floor and ate an apple with my dog. I guess my mom was right that things were going to get tighter. I didn't know we wouldn't be able to have the fucking lights on, though.

———

April 13, 2008:

I had an awesome 20th birthday. I am not sure if I know what happens after you die, but I do know Jonny said happy birthday to me. Listen to this.

I got to work the morning of my birthday and one of the guys comes up to me and says, "For your birthday, I'm going to show you a magic trick." At first I was like, "Umm, I turned 20, not 5," but anyway I let him go. He folds up a $5 bill in a cone shape and looks at me and says, "In life, you may not always have money . . . ," he proceeds to pull out a rainbow-colored handkerchief from the $5 bill and continues, "but you will always have your rainbows"—and then hands me a rainbow-colored Beanie Baby.

He was laughing and smiling, waiting for me to praise him for his silly magic trick. I stared at him speechless with my jaw down to the floor. A tear rolled down my face. I was stunned. Slowly and distraught, I asked, "Why did you just say that to me?" He looked back at me confused, having no idea anything about me or what I had been through over the last 10 months. He shrugged and said, "Gee, sorry, Hil, it was just a trick." He walked away and there I was, alone, staring into thin air, holding a rainbow Beanie Baby and a rainbow handkerchief.

This stranger had no idea my friend had passed away; he had no idea what I had looked for and felt when I saw rainbows. And he surely had no idea that over the last few weeks I was unable to make doctors' appointments, turn my lights on, OR that I was working at this fucking job BECAUSE I had no money. Yet this random man decides to tell me that in life I may not always have money, but I will always have my rainbows?!?! I excused myself and went outside to smoke a cigarette. I looked up at the sky and said, "Thank you."

I got back upstairs to my office and another coworker comes up to me and says he wants to take me to lunch for my birthday. What's the kid's name? Johnny. Of course, it is.

We went out to eat, and when I got back to the office, my boss told me he had to speak to me in the conference room. I thought I was getting fired. I walk in and the entire staff was in there with a birthday cake. Everyone sang happy birthday. I go to blow my candles out, what was on the cake? A rainbow.

13

THE 20-YEAR SECRET

Over the next few months, I worked my ass off to save as much money as I could to get back to Albany. I opened a bank account that would be my rent fund. This way once I got back to school, my house money was in a safe place that *I* was in control of—not my parents.

I made sure I did well enough in my night classes to earn the credits I needed and ended up paying my genius little brother $50 per test to pass my online exams for me. He was only 14 but passed my college courses with ease. As the summer of 2008 came to an end, I told my boss that I was going back to school. He wanted me to stay with the company and offered me a permanent position. I was flattered but basically laughed in his face. There was *no* chance I wasn't going back to college!

August 22, 2008:

    I can't believe tonight is my first night back in Albany! I can't believe I am here! I actually did it! I have been waiting eight months for this moment. I don't think it has hit me yet that I am in my new home with my best friends, far away from my parents' chaotic drama. Do most divorces last this long? Seems like seven years is a long time for a divorce to drag on, and frankly I am getting sick of it. I am proud of myself for working these last eight months to pay and earn my *way back to college. The day before I came up here I got a letter in the mail from my dentist saying I owe them $1,760. HAHAHA, nice parting gift. I think the universe is testing me sometimes. More dentist and money problems. What else is new? At least I am up here now where I don't have to worry about that too much. I am looking forward to starting over. I'm so proud of myself for making my way back to college.*

At this moment, I was looking forward to starting over. I didn't know, though, just how much would start over for me.

––––––––

September 14, 2008:

Two days ago I woke up to a text from my dad saying, "I tried to be a good dad and I am sorry for everything but I am at the end of my rope." He has been using these suicidal texts as ploys to get me to call him if I go a few weeks without speaking to him. And let's be real, has he really tried to be a good dad? If he did, it was a shitty effort.

I know his suicidal texts are bullshit, but since I am a human I can't help but be concerned, so I tried to reach him. He didn't answer. Then I get a text from Brock saying, "I think Dad is going to kill himself." I called Brock and he said no one knew where our dad was. The sad part is, there isn't really anyone to call.

A few hours later Brock said they found my dad and he was totally fine. Why does my dad keep doing this shit to us? It's annoying how complicated our relationship is. I wish it didn't weigh so much on Brock's and my shoulders. I feel like I am at the end of my rope. I'm sick of being tricked into these phone calls. I just want to live my life. I didn't work for eight months to get back to college just to deal with his baby bullshit. I don't know if I can deal with it anymore.

I know my mom doesn't like hearing about my dad, but I called her anyway. I was saying to her that I wasn't sure if I could maintain a relationship with my dad anymore because of how detrimental it is to my life. I feel like it's a chore. He is constantly making us feel like he is going to do something bad to himself so we will reach out. It's exhausting. My mom told me I need to cut him out of my life for good. I kept saying, "Mom, what am I supposed to do? He's my dad. He made me."

I don't know why I used that phrase, but I kept saying it to her, "He made me." Finally, my mom told me she was coming up to Albany this weekend so we could have lunch together. That was weird.

"Mom, why would you drive three hours to come have lunch?"

She told me we had to talk and she thought it would be better to speak in person.

"Mom, you're being weird—what is going on? If you have to tell me something so important, you can tell me now over the phone." At this point I was in my bedroom alone, and my roommates were watching TV in the living room.

THEN CAME THE 20-YEAR-OLD SECRET. . . .

My mom told me to sit down, so I did. She took a deep breath and said, "Hil, listen, that man did NOT make you. He is NOT your biological father. When we were first married and tried to have kids, we found out your dad was sterile. We decided to use sperm donors, and you and Brock do not have the same biological father. No one was ever supposed to know, just me, him, and both of our moms. I'm so sorry."

My heart sank into my stomach. I stared at myself in the mirror, realizing in that second that my whole life has been somewhat of a lie. My mouth was wide open. I couldn't shut it—it was involuntary. I literally couldn't shut it. I was speechless and confused. Finally I said, "Mom, are you serious?! You fucking wait until NOW to tell me this?!"

She told me she was so sorry and that she didn't know if she would ever tell me, but things had gotten so bad and once she realized I was holding on to this destructive relationship just because I thought "he made me," she needed me to know that he actually did not make me.

I stayed silent on the phone for a few minutes. I wasn't sure what to say. Then I started freaking out. "Did he adopt me? What nationality am I? Do I have brothers and sisters? Who the hell is my dad?"

My mom doesn't have any answers about my biological father and told me I won't be able to get any information about him since he was an anonymous donor. She told me that she doesn't want to tell Brock since he is too young. I told her there was ZERO chance I would ever keep this from him. We finally agreed that when I come home for the Jewish holidays next week we will sit down and tell Brock together. My mom kept asking if I was okay and I told her I needed a drink and to sit and think. We hung up and I called Jen.

"Hey, mama!" Jen answered happily.

"Jen, sit down."

She was like, "Oh my God, Hil, who died?" Sadly we have gotten too many calls about people dying. I told her no one, but that she had to sit down. I proceeded to tell her the news that I was just told.

Jen was quiet for a minute, and then she started hysterically laughing. "I knew you were a mailman baby! I knew you were not like him! I told you from the moment I met him that you were not like him!"

Jen made me laugh, but I was still in a daze. After the first time she met my dad she would always call me a "mailman baby." She was confident my mom had an affair with a mailman since Jen was certain I was not my dad's child. I told Jen this was not the time to joke and this was serious. She said, "Hil, it's not funny, but it is kind of amazing—you aren't anything like him, and now you know you won't inherit any of his fucked-up traits."

Jen is right. I feel a weird sense of relief. I am also scared. Jen and I hung up and I finally left my room after two hours of being in there. I walked to the living room, where my girls still were. They asked me what was wrong; they could see it on my face. I told them what had just happened. I walked into my bedroom to have a normal conversation with my mom, and I walked out of my bedroom knowing my dad isn't even my dad. None of my girls knew what to say, so they rolled me a joint, poured me a drink, and said, "Well, this is going to be a great chapter in your book."

It's hard to admit I kind of do feel relief. Is that messed up? It's also comforting to know that I don't have any genetic predispositions to his psychotic bullshit. This just opened up so many doors, though I don't have a clue what is going to happen next. Maybe the chapter of my book will be "The 20-Year Secret." I keep reminding myself—be not afraid.

Now starts the hunt for information. Let's see if I can find out who my real dad is.

14

THE SECRET AFTERMATH

Over the next few days, I walked around feeling confused and unsure of who I really was. I was trying to navigate this new "after," dealing with the reality that I believed my whole life my dad was my father . . . and he wasn't! I tried to remain strong, but every minute I thought of a new question about my biological father. I was not okay with the fact that I would never know who he was. It was an unsettling feeling and made me feel incomplete and anxious. I was also trying to understand why my mom had waited until now to tell me, since things had been bad with my dad for so long.

I called my grandma to talk to her and told her I knew the secret. She immediately knew what I was referring to; there was only *one* secret. Just like my mom had said, Grandma reiterated that they had never thought our situation would get to where it was and they had never intended to tell us the truth. I kept saying, "I just hope my dad is a good guy, whoever he is." Grandma assured me that based on how I ended up, she knew my dad, whoever he was, was a good man.

My mom called to check in and make sure I was doing okay. I joked that when I got back home, I had to go see my therapist and said, "Dr. K. is going to get a kick out of this!"

My mom then told me that Dr. K. had known for years. I felt like the wind had been knocked out of me. *What do you mean, he's known for years?*

She told me that when things had started to get really bad with my dad, she'd called Dr. K. to tell him and his advice was *not* to tell me. Every ounce of me felt completely betrayed by him. For years I sat in his office pouring my heart out about our fucked-up relationship, and the whole time, he knew my "dad" wasn't even my dad?

The next time I was on Long Island, I went to Dr. K.'s office and confronted him. I was infuriated and couldn't believe that someone I'd trusted so much had hidden this from me. His response was, "Hil, why does it matter if he is your biological father or not? You were still going through this with him, and he was still your dad."

It did matter. It mattered to me. I didn't agree with him at all. Maybe in his mind he felt justified in keeping this from me, but I was looking at it from another perspective. I kept thinking, *What else do you know that you are hiding from me?* I appreciate all the help he gave me through my teens, but I was never able to trust him again, and our relationship ended shortly thereafter. Talk about feeling "abandoned."

————

During the "secret aftermath" I was freaking out over my medical history. I called my doctor and said I had to see him right away. I needed him to know my whole life I'd been telling him my dad's medical history and I actually didn't even know my *real* dad's medical history! *What if my biological father died at 30? How am I supposed to know if cancer runs in my genes and I'm going to die soon?* My anxiety was through the roof over this. I reminded myself to Be Not Afraid.

September 16, 2008:

I'm doing things to keep busy because thinking about this situation is making me go nuts. My dad is going to go CRAZY if he finds out I know he is not my dad. For now I am not going to tell him I know. It's going to be so weird to start telling my friends from back home the truth, like, "Oh yeah, guys, forgot to mention that I just found out my dad isn't my dad after all!" Crazy. I have been saying forever that the only thing my dad passed down to me is his temper. Now, knowing that is impossible, it's hard for me to accept that it was a result of my environment. I really can't believe he isn't my biological father. I feel like a lot of my life has been a lie. I am NOT going to see him when I am home for the holidays. I need some time to think. It's freaking me out that I may have siblings somewhere out there. I wonder what they would be like. Would we look alike? I guess I'll never know.

———

I was really nervous as to how Brock was going to react to the big secret. I was worried that he was going to be distraught over the news. *He is only 14. How could he not be?* I wanted to make sure someone at his school knew this unusual situation we were going through, just in case his grades or behavior started to change. I had kept in touch with my high school guidance counselor, Chris Safina, who still worked at the school, so I contacted him and told him the story. He appreciated the heads-up and could hardly believe the truth, considering he had helped me through so much and had been there for me when Child Protective Services would show up to speak to me.

When I got home, I told my mom I had decided I wanted to tell Brock alone. She wasn't thrilled about this but ultimately said it was fine. I told Brock we were going to spend the evening together. I took him to get a haircut and grab a bite to eat.

At the restaurant I said, "Brock, I need to tell you something pretty serious."

"What's up?"

"I just found something out about our family I need you to know. This will not change anything between us, and it's okay if you get upset. Dad is not our biological father. He was unable to have children. We are sperm donor babies and have different dads."

My heart was pounding. I was so nervous as to what kind of reaction was about to detonate out of my little brother.

"Yeah, I figured that out about 2 years ago," he said nonchalantly while finishing his bite.

I scrutinized his reaction. I was speechless. This was not what I was expecting.

"Brock, 2 years ago you were 12 years old. What do you mean you figured this out?"

Brock proceeded to tell me that 2 years prior, he and my dad had gotten into a fight and my dad had gone nuts and stormed out of the house. Brock then went downstairs and started looking at family pictures and realized that we look nothing like my dad's side of the family and for the most part, we aren't anything like them. He said he just knew deep down we weren't my dad's kids.

I was floored by this. I was anticipating an emotional explosion of confusion and anger. Instead, he barely took his eyes off his dinner plate while casually telling me he somehow knew this all along.

"Brock, why didn't you talk to me about this then? Are you okay?"

"Hil, you would have told me it was wishful thinking and of course we are his kids but just got Mom's genes. And yes, I am okay. Good news is we won't turn out to be crazy like him."

I leaned over the table and gave him a hug. Honestly, he was right, and that probably was how I would have reacted if at 12 years old he had randomly told me he thought we weren't my dad's children. I told Brock that even though we didn't have the same dad, we were still 100 percent siblings and our relationship would never, *ever* change.

He looked at me and, like a typical 14-year-old smart-ass, said, "Are you mad that I got the smart sperm?"

I laughed and told him he was a jerk. I also told him I had given his school a heads-up on the situation.

"Damn, bro! I was really thinking you were going to lose your shit over this!"

15

MY FOREVER HAZE OF: HE DIDN'T MAKE YOU

The day the 20-year secret was revealed, I walked into my bedroom angry and upset and wanted to talk to my mom about the man I thought of as my dad. I walked out of my bedroom in a new Forever Haze of *After*, knowing that man was actually not my dad.

I spent days doing a lot of soul-searching after finding out the secret. My whole life I had been holding on to this toxic relationship all because I thought I somehow owed it to him, since he was my dad, and he'd created me. Now that I knew this wasn't the case, I had to find a new reason or excuse to hold on to him.

I realized that the root of my problems with my dad was that I was expecting too much from him. The reality was, he was not able to give me the fatherly care I had always wanted. I realized that instead of talking to him like an adult and trying to rely on him as a dad, which always resulted in fights and me being angry and disappointed, perhaps I should speak to him as if he was a child, knowing he was mentally sick and unable to connect with me the way I wanted.

This was a game changer. Going forward, I became very superficial with him. I stopped telling him details of my life and stopped expecting him to react or give me input like typical dads do. Once my conversations with him became more like this, I became less and less angry. Now I wasn't getting disappointed, because I stopped expecting him to do the right thing. The less he knew about me, the fewer opportunities he had to make my life more difficult.

I would spend years curious about the kind of man who had created the other half of me. *Is he a good person? Is he a piece of shit? Is he even alive? Do I have siblings? Do they look like me?*

My mom and Jen told me to cut my dad out of my life for good, but I wasn't strong enough to do it. Part of me felt bad for him. I knew he wasn't right in his mind and that something was off with him. I guess, like my therapist said, I hated feeling abandoned—and I didn't want to be the one doing the abandonment. So, this was the compromise I made. I still maintained a relationship, but I took the emotional aspect out of it.

The reality is, DNA or not, if it weren't for him, I wouldn't be me.

16

THE FOREVER HAZE OF AFTER

On Christmas Eve of 2008, my mom, Brock, and I had dinner together, and Mom told me she had a present for me. She went on to say that it had been hard for her to see my friends and me deal with Jon's death the year before and she had been working on something all this time. She had known my friends since we were young; all of us had been close since elementary school, and she had watched us grow up. She went from seeing us as young kids to watching us deal with an unimaginable situation when Jon died.

My mom handed me her beautiful present, and as I read it, my eyes filled with tears.

Jon's Friends

In a split second between "before" and "after," the girls
found skirts that weren't too short, tops that
weren't too low and heels that weren't too high,
and classically accessorized with tear-shadowed eyes and earnest,
earthbound young men in dark suits.
Gravity once had no hold on them, and they soared, buoyed
by the worldly innocence unique to their age. When it was "before,"

they swarmed, confident the elements were theirs to command
by the powers vested in their brash youth and raucous laughter.

Just yesterday, in a now-classic rite of passage, dressed in
their mothers' sheets they pretended to be Greek aristocracy,
laughed under the mid-summer moon,
and in the honeysuckle and lilac-scented night scraped one of their own off the
pavement.
A moment ago they saw no further than their next kiss,
now they stare at the future and mortality
carves shadows in their cheeks.
In the forever-haze of "after," whispering over
wrinkled photos they try to make sense
of the senseless.
Their hero,
fallen,
they create new rituals for their new reality
with candles and sidewalk altars where
they congregate softly vigilant and count the days—
One, two, three—until he
will rise again,
But he will appear to the chosen only
In dreams and rainbows.

R. Gerson, December 10, 2008

Everyone talks about a moment that changes their life, but my mom gave it a name. My mom called it the Forever Haze of *After*. I always knew I would write a book, but I'd never been able to think of a title. When I read the words "in the forever-haze of after," I immediately knew that was it. This poem meant more to me than I can ever explain.

Thank you so much, Mom.

17

CHRISTMAS DAY: NEGATIVE $109,000?!

On Christmas Day 2008, I had plans to go to the home of the guy I was dating at the time—I'll call him Mark—to meet his family. On the way to Mark's, I stopped at 7-Eleven to grab dessert so I wouldn't show up empty-handed. I went to the cash register and my card got declined. I told them that was a mistake and to try again—declined. I left with no dessert.

What a great impression this is going to be! I knew I didn't have a lot of money, but I should have had the $8 in my account for the cake I wanted to bring. I got to Mark's house and introduced myself to his family. I excused myself and asked if I could use his computer.

I logged onto my bank account, and as soon as I saw the screen I felt dizzy. The room was closing in on me. I thought I was going to pass out. My balance read "(–$109,000.00)."

WHAT THE FUCK?! NEGATIVE ONE HUNDRED NINE THOUSAND DOLLARS???

This made no sense. I panicked and called my mom. "Mom, what the hell is going on? My bank account says I am negative $109,000!"

"What? Honey, this must be some kind of mistake. Why don't you stop by and I'll give you some cash. No banks are open because it's Christmas. We can work this out in a few days."

December 25, 2008:

　　When I got home tonight my mom told me she was going to try and take care of the bank situation over the phone and asked for my log-in information. I said, "Mom, we aren't in $109,000 debt, right?" She told me no and she would figure it out. I know something shady is going on, and I know this is going to be an issue because shit like this always happens to me. I'm not even surprised. $109,000— that is a LOT of money. Happy holidays to me.

A few days later, Mark and I ended things. *That was fast! Maybe I should have brought some dessert.* My relationships never ended up getting too serious. I always found guys who were broken in one way or another. Dr. K. used to tell me I tried to save everyone and was drawn to people who needed help. Maybe he was right.

December 29, 2008:

　　The negative $109,000 was no mistake. I woke up and Mom explained that she owes her lawyers over $54,000. Even though their agreement says she doesn't have to pay them until she sells the house when Brock graduates high school, apparently the lawyers entered a court order to collect the money . . . now —and since my mom's name is on my bank account, they doubled the amount owed and froze my account—<u>MY</u> account is the key. Mom had to take my 14-year-old brother to the bank to have him sign papers to pull all his bar mitzvah money out of his account. She had to cancel all bank accounts that had her name on them—all credit cards, everything. She did this so if the lawyers go after any other accounts, there won't be any money in them. I haven't even been able to drive down my block in my car because my mom thinks they will repossess it, since her name is on the loan. My car has been backed into Jen's driveway for the past three days so hopefully no one can find it. Mom switched cars with my aunt. This way if the tow truck comes to our house, they can't take someone's car that doesn't have her name on the registration. Is this normal??? Are they going to come after my house? Or anything in it? Not like they have much furniture to take, since my dad already took all of that, but is this normal?

———

After the New Year, I was going to be home for a few more weeks until winter break was over. Jen left for a semester abroad in Barcelona, and I needed to stay busy since my best friend was now on the other side of the world. I literally had *no* money because of my bank account situation and needed to figure out a way to get cash. I hadn't spoken to my dad in weeks, but one night I had a dream about him and sure enough, the next day he called wanting to see me.

I refused to tell him about the negative $109,000 because I knew he would get a sick kick out of the situation. Whereas my mom taught me not to kick a man when he was down, my dad enjoyed doing so. He'd always get some sense of satisfaction from hearing that my mom and I were struggling.

It turns out the only reason he called was so I could meet one of his newest girlfriends. Anytime a new woman was in the picture, he tried to rekindle our relationship so the woman thought we had one.

When I showed up to see him, after a brief chat, he casually asked me if I could get them weed. I was surprised. I didn't even know my dad smoked. This was the first time he had asked me something like this, but I saw an opportunity for myself. Since I had no money, which I partially blamed on him because he was the reason my mom owed the lawyers so much, I figured I would overcharge him to make extra cash. At one point he mentioned he had a bottle of painkillers upstairs he wasn't taking. I asked if I could have them. He didn't ask me any questions and handed me a bottle with 50 oxycodone.

I sold them all in 24 hours and put the money aside so I could have some cash to float me until my bank account was figured out. I was always so good at selling drugs, I told myself that my biological father had to have been a drug dealer. My dad continued to buy weed from me until I went back to school, and I continued to overcharge him, telling myself that I was getting some of the child support he owed my mom. I think deep down he really thought we were maintaining some sort of a relationship, since I was seeing him more frequently once he started picking up from me. I was in it for the money, as usual.

———

A few weeks later, I was back at Albany. My mom was able to resolve the money situation, and her lawyers removed the hold on my account. But now, a different set of lawyers were about to mess up my day.

February 5, 2009:

Holy shit. I just got a call from my mom. "Hil, we're in family court and your father won't admit you're back being a full-time student and working part-time. You need to call this number back in 5 minutes." She gave me a phone number and hung up the phone. "What the hell is going on?" I thought. I called back the number, gave them my name, and was told I was about to be put on speakerphone in front of the courtroom. UMMMM . . . WHAT?! I was just cross-examined for 13 minutes back and forth between my mom and dad's lawyers asking me questions! They even made me raise my right hand and take an oath, WHILE I AM LYING IN MY BED AT COLLEGE IN ALBANY. I should have never had to do what I just did. I am so fucking pissed at my parents.

Somehow, this situation really happened. I remember the judge telling me over the phone to raise my right hand. Now try and picture this—I am 20 years old at college, in my bedroom, and a judge tells me to raise my right hand to swear an oath—while I am 180 miles away from the courtroom! I don't know how this was legitimate. I really did raise my right hand like an idiot. I was confused, but while I was swearing the oath I put my middle finger up. *Fuck you all.*

My parents were at court fighting over child support, again. My mom was trying to get my dad to start paying child support for me, since the courts never revisited our case when I returned to school. For whatever reason, the judge insisted on talking to me directly.

I was infuriated. My dad's lawyer was *such* a dick. He would ask me a question: "Hilary, were you a full-time student during this time period?"

"Well, no, but I was—," then he would cut me off.

"Hilary, this is a yes-or-no answer."

This guy was a real asshole. I was trying to explain that the whole reason I withdrew in the first place was because *his client* wasn't paying my mom child support or helping me pay for school, so I withdrew so I could pay for my own college. But no one seemed to care. Even when I returned to being a full-time student, my dad was able to go months without paying my mom, and he received zero consequences. His lawyer wasn't even asking me about being back at school; he was focusing on the fact that I withdrew, trying to make me out like I was a shitty kid, and it wasn't even why they were in court in the first place.

I contemplated screaming through the phone, "HE ISN'T PAYING CHILD SUPPORT BUT HE IS BUYING DRUGS FROM ME!" But instead, I just let the lawyers make me feel like a worthless piece of shit.

My unfortunate experiences with family court showed me that the best interest of the kids is not always at the forefront. Typically, the more expensive lawyer gets what's best for their client. In my situation, that client was my dad.

18

THE BOY WHO CRIED WOLF

February 11, 2009:

Today in my child development class we had an entire discussion about nature versus nurture and things got kinda personal. I'm like a walking experiment, so when some girl said it's all genetics that affect your temperament, I chimed in. I told her I completely disagreed. I said that I hadn't found out until recently that one of my parents wasn't my biological one, so any traits I thought I got from them weren't from the genes, they were from the environment. This girl replies and says, "Well, couldn't it be that your biological parent had a similar temperament to the one that raised you?" I got so pissed. This girl doesn't even know me and didn't even care that my world was turned upside down by this news. And I was mad that she asked me this question, maybe because I'd never thought about it. Could you imagine if my biological father actually was like my dad? What a bummer that would be. But since I will never know the answer, I said, "I don't know, why don't you call the fucking sperm bank!"

———

Sometime in the next few months, my dad told Brock and me that he was moving to Florida. At first we didn't believe him. It didn't make sense to us that he'd leave. He loved having control and power, and once he moved, those things would be harder to maintain.

Before my dad moved, my brother "slipped" and told him that we knew he wasn't our biological father. My dad lost it. He said our mom was lying and he was going to prove it. Not only was his control and power slipping away because he was moving, but now he knew that we knew the secret. What he didn't know was that I was making arrangements to get information from the sperm bank.

Once my dad was down in Florida for good, my brother and I distanced ourselves from him. If we stopped answering him for too long, we would get texts that he was suffering from one illness or another. When he lived in New York and we didn't answer him, he sent us suicidal text messages. Now he was dying every other week. Sometimes it was cancer, brain tumors, brain bleeding, lung issues, blood clots, internal bleeding—you name it, he had it. When this first started, Brock and I would get worried and call him immediately. He'd get emotional and tell us how much he loved us and wanted to rebuild our relationships, but at this point it was too little too late. He would give us botched-up details about the illness that never made sense. We'd talk for a week or so, checking in to see how he was doing, and then return to our normal lives.

Before we knew it, we'd get another text about another disease. I couldn't understand how he was suddenly getting sick so often and then the sicknesses would miraculously disappear. I did some research, spoke to a few of my psychology professors, and learned about Munchausen syndrome. It's a mental disorder that causes a person to act as if he or she has an illness when he or she is not really sick. People like this have severe emotional difficulties.

Unfortunately, my dad is the boy who cried wolf. Brock and I always knew that we'd never know when he was telling the truth, but one day, he would be.

Since I started writing this book, I learned that my dad has stage IV metastatic cancer and likely won't live longer than a year. Of course, at first I didn't believe him. But after speaking to his girlfriend and confirming with the hospital, I know this time it's real. The irony of finding out he is dying during the few months I finally found the courage to fulfill my dream and write this book has not been lost on me.

Brock and I weren't sure how to deal with the news. At first, we felt a tinge of guilt that we didn't initially believe him—but how could we? After years of lies and exaggerations over health issues, we thought this was just another one.

Since his diagnosis, my dad has called me many times and has been overwhelmingly emotional and remorseful for what he did to my brother and me during our childhood. Sometimes it takes the scare of death for people to realize how badly they screwed up. Being apologetic now does not change what he did to us, and I could never forgive someone for hurting my mom the way that he did. I feel sorry for him that he didn't live a life full of love or meaningful relationships. Instead, his life was full of loneliness and anger. I know having cancer is scary, and as a human being, I don't want anyone to suffer. The best I can do for him is let him know that even though I should hate him, I don't. I'm in too good a place in my life to carry hatred around. I will let him die in peace so that once he does, I can feel in my heart I did the right thing.

19
_____

"HERE HE IS, I LOVE YOU!"

After the big secret was revealed, my mom contacted the sperm donor agency and requested information on my donor. I made it clear I wanted any information I could get. The agency said all they could provide was a copy of the donor's application, but nothing else. They told us that due to anonymity laws, I would never find him.

October 20, 2009:

    It's been a little over a year since I found out my dad is not my biological father, but now, the information has finally arrived. I am writing this diary entry on my phone while I'm at Amanda's decorating for our friend's 21st birthday party. My mom just called to tell me the sperm bank sent her the information and she's gonna email it to me when she gets home—I almost dropped the streamers I was helping hang up. I know this is what I asked for, but it's strange to know I am going to open an email that will reveal to me where half my genes came from, where half of me came from. I'm nervous I guess but excited at the same time—kinda just freaking out that this day has arrived. For the past year I have been asking myself every day when I would find out this information, and here I am sitting at my friend's house waiting for the email. Since we are partying tonight I don't think it's a good idea for me to open it while I'm drunk, since I have no idea how I will react. Jen wants me to wait until

80

the morning and read it while I'm on the phone with her—I think that's my best bet.

————

October 22, 2009:

So yesterday morning after I was done throwing up from Skippy and was able to lift my head off my pillow, I opened the email my mom had sent me that revealed to me information on the man that made me, whom I have never met, never even known existed for the first 20 years of my life. My mom's subject of the email was "Here he is, I love you!"—it made me laugh. The attachment was labeled "C380," which was his donor code. I guess that will be his name from now on, my dad—C380. The application had some basic characteristics: He was born in 1963, he was 6 feet tall, 160 pounds—hazel eyes, curly brown hair, fair skin—other than me only being 5'1", I guess I got some of his genes, huh? His religion was Jewish, so I'm not Italian like I thought. The form says he was married and going to school to be a dentist. I hate the dentist—ironic that I've had all these dental insurance problems over the past few years, can't even afford a cavity filling, and this guy is a dentist. Of course, he is.

On the second page, the date of the application is filled in as 10/7/86—and all it says about his birthday is that he was born in 1963, so he was about 23 when he filled it out. I was joking with Amanda and said, "He filled this out in 1986, I wasn't born until 1988—that means half of me lived in a refrigerator for the first 2 years of my existence!"

I'm sure he needed to raise some money to get through school, so why not donate some sperm? And no doubt, because here I am. . . . So thanks, C380! I wonder if he has this clairvoyant, dreams come true trait. Maybe that's where I get it from. There's a section for medical history and the only things crossed off were "hay fever" and "allergies." I freaked out and was like, "Oh shit, I have hay fever disease," but then I looked it up and it's some type of allergies, so I'm fine with that. No other major medical conditions were checked, but he was so young when he did the application. I am still nervous that maybe some shit runs in his family that I should know about.

I wonder what he looks like. I think it would be cool to see a picture of him, to see if I look like him at all. I wonder if he's got kids now. That would mean I'd *have biological half-siblings somewhere around the world, wherever he is. I wonder if he's even alive. Maybe he's a wealthy dentist—how ironic and funny would that be? Or maybe he lied on the application and is actually a drug lord, and that is why I am so good at selling drugs! Who knows. At this point, I feel like I know the same amount about him as I do my other "dad." Basically nothing, just surface shit.*

I haven't spoken to my dad in like a month. He's still unemployed in Florida and his checks ran out so he's not giving my mom child support, so she's down an extra $600 a month. I thought it was going to get easier when he moved, but the struggles just keep continuing. . . . Looking forward to the day when I can put them to an end.

20

GEARING UP FOR GRADUATION

In January of 2010, I received a call from Jonny's parents, who told me our high school was giving a scholarship in Jon's name to a senior football player. They asked me if I would deliver a speech at the award ceremony prior to the scholarship recipient being announced. I was honored.

January 26, 2010:

Like when I wrote Jon's eulogy, I sat in Jen's bedroom alone with a pack of cigarettes to write his scholarship speech. I called Jon's parents and my guy friends and asked them what they thought of Jonny as an athlete. I took notes of things they were saying so I could include their direct quotes. Some of my friends attended the ceremony and sat with Jon's parents. My brother is on the football team, so it was special to have him and my mom there to support me as well.

I was nervous to speak in front of 300 people, so Jen planned on standing across from the podium to give me hand cues if I was going too slow or too fast. First two lines I said, I looked up and she was already crying—so that plan was ruined. During the speech I told the football players that Jonny had been a leader on and off the field; that he looked at his teammates as brothers no matter how good they were or what they looked like, and he accepted everyone as his teammates and family. I told them that Jonny preferred watching college football over the NFL because he'd say that college ball was more about heart and less about the money. I told them that Jon did not get the opportunity to fulfill his dreams but that they can fulfill theirs, and that if they are the recipient of his scholarship, they should play with him in their minds and hearts. I told them to never let the odds keep them from pursuing what they know in their hearts they were meant to do.

When I got up there and started speaking—everything stopped. My friend took a video and you can literally hear a pin drop. She filmed the football players, and to tell you the truth, that was the only time I got emotional when I watched it—to see how focused they were and how much they were really listening to me. I can only hope the message got out to at least one kid sitting there. I hope they realize that life is short and it's important to fulfill your dreams, something Jonny wasn't able to do. The waiters even stopped serving dinner to listen to me. I hope Jonny liked it. I did it for him.

———

A few days after the scholarship ceremony I returned to Albany to gear up for graduation. I couldn't believe my time there was ending. Every semester while at college, I had a job to pay my way through school. I felt a sense of pride knowing I had worked and earned my way toward a degree. My last semester I got a 4.0 GPA thanks to hard work, good friends who studied with me, and my Adderall prescription.

My dad and I were barely speaking, but I was okay with him being in Florida far away from me. I hadn't spoken to him in over a month, but right before graduation he called to tell me how proud he was and that he wanted to come to my graduation. He hadn't told me he was proud of me, well, ever? Part of me didn't believe him. I didn't even know if he knew what I majored in. He never acted like a dad, he didn't help me get through college, in fact he made it harder for me, and now, conveniently right before I graduated, he was proud?

He asked if I wanted him to book a flight to come to my gradua-tion. I immediately caught on to what he was doing—I'd seen this before. He knew there was no way he could be in the same room as my mom. He asked me if he could come because he knew I would say no, and then I would be the bad guy, not him. He manipulated situations like this all the time.

———

About the same time, my mom told me that her boyfriend, Steven, was moving in. My mom and he were high school sweethearts but had gone on to marry other people. I liked Steven because he really stepped up for my mom and brother. Brock was in high school when he and my mom were dating, and Steven would be at Brock's sports games and take him fishing. He taught Brock how to drive. I was happy that my mom was in a relationship with someone who really cared, and I was happy that Brock had a solid father figure in his life, something I missed out on.

If I am being honest, I was uneasy about Steven moving into my house while I was at college. I knew I would be graduating in a few months and when I returned home, he would already be settled in. It was nothing personal against him, but I thought it would be weird to have a man in the house after years and years of it just being my mom, Brock, and me.

It turned out to be fine, and to this day, my mom and Steven are still happily living together. I would later find out that ending up with your high school sweetheart runs in the family.

———

April came around and my friends threw me a surprise party for my 22nd birthday. Jen came up to help them plan it, and before the party she handed me a huge box. When I opened it, there was a fireproof safe with the words "The Forever Haze of After" engraved on it. In the safe were copies of Jon's eulogy, the scholarship speech I had written, my mom's poem, letters I had written to Jen, writing supplies, USB drives, highlighters, etc. Then she handed me another big box. Inside was a massive binder, filled with copies of all the digital diary entries I had written, tabbed by month, date, and year. She had written me a note: "Now you have everything organized and zero excuses. Share your story and write your fucking book! I love you!"

The gift made me incredibly emotional. I couldn't believe how much time, effort, and thought she had put into this. She had asked me for copies of my diary entries a few months back and promised me she was working on something and wouldn't read them. I trusted Jen with my life, so I sent them to her, not totally sure what she was doing, but certain my deepest secrets were in good hands. This was the most meaningful present I have ever received in my entire life. It was a major factor in how organized and structured I had all my materials to effectively write this book, even though I waited 10 years!

A few days later a package arrived from my dad. He texted me and told me a birthday present was on the way. I opened the package and out fell eight packs of cigarettes. There wasn't even a birthday card.

21

POSTGRADUATION

Returning to my mom's house after graduation was certainly an adjustment. I had been on my own for so long, hadn't had to answer to anyone, and now I was back to sharing a wall with my mom, *and* Steven.

I graduated from college with a major in psychology and a double minor in criminal justice and sociology. I still wanted to help juveniles, but I needed a master's degree and couldn't afford graduate school. My mom encouraged me to work for a nonprofit organization because I always became so passionate when I volunteered for charity events, which I did whenever I had an opportunity. For years, I was obsessed with Oprah and Ellen. Watching them change people's lives by simply giving them money, a car, or a scholarship for college always made me emotional. My dream job would have been to be the person who found them the people who needed help.

Sometimes I would come up with charity ideas and devise a whole business plan. One time it was a food-drive contest among all Long Island high schools. Each school would pick a local shelter or organization, and whatever food they collected would go to the organization. Whichever high school collected the most food would receive a private concert by a big-time celebrity who grew up on the Island.

Another time I thought of a college-loan program after I was denied a $3,000 loan to help pay for my textbooks. In the same week, I saw my roommate Sam get $20,000 wired into her account when her grandparents cosigned a loan for her because they didn't want her to have to work during her senior year. I was beyond frustrated when this happened. I was a good student, on my way to earning a 4.0, was working 20 hours a week with preschoolers with disabilities on top of taking full-time classes—and all because my parents were broke, fighting, and unable to cosign a loan for me, I was given zero help.

My idea was that local malls could start a program where they gave colleges small "donations" before the beginning of the school year. Those donations would be put into a fund so students like me, who couldn't get small institutional loans, could get money from that fund if we met certain academic criteria. Then, when a store needed to hire people during busy times or holiday seasons, they would instead contact the school, which would send a student who had received money from the fund to work to pay off their loan. It would have been an incentive for the businesses, since they wouldn't have had to hire anyone and would have gotten a tax write-off, and for the school, since they would have been able to help more students. Win-win.

I couldn't find any nonprofit jobs that paid well enough, so I started working with Jen at the bar in an upscale off-track betting location, where rich men bet a lot of money on horses. They would tip us $20 after we brought them a $2.50 soda. I was making great money, sometimes $500 to $700 a day in cash tips.

One day when I was working at the OTB, my coworker's friend passed away. I think he committed suicide, but I can't remember for sure. During a conversation, she told me her friend's mom was upset because she needed to raise $1,000 to participate in an awareness walk in honor of her son, but she didn't have the money. I looked around our job, seeing men bet up to $10,000 on a horse. When my coworker left for the day, I went from seat to seat collecting money from the gamblers.

I'd say, "How much did you just bet on that race? $500? And you can't give me $50 to help a woman who just lost her son?" I laid it on even harder on the VIP customers who were betting thousands of dollars on a fucking long shot. By the end of the weekend, I raised the thousand bucks. The following week I handed my coworker an envelope with the money and said, "Give this to your friend's mom so she can walk in honor of her son. Tell her I'm sorry for her loss."

My coworker looked at me, startled that I would do this when I didn't even know the guy who had passed away, let alone his mom. Her eyes filled with tears.

"Hil, thank you so much. I cannot believe you did that."

I couldn't believe no one else had.

To me, it made no sense that someone in a position to help someone else wouldn't. I think since my mom and I struggled so much financially, sometimes I didn't understand why people (other than my grandma) weren't helping us. I told myself my whole life that if I ever was in a position to help someone else, I would undoubtedly. So, I did what I could, when I could.

I'd find out a few years later, the passion to help others in need ran through my blood.

22

ANDREW

A few weeks after I got home from college, Andrew called to check in. We always kept in touch, and knowing I was back in town, he wanted to hang out. We set up a date to go to the beach to catch up.

Andrew picked me up that morning and we sat at the beach, drinking and laughing, talking about the last year of our lives. We related to each other on a deeper level than most people. His dad died when Andrew was five years old, so neither of us grew up with a father figure and we were both raised by single moms. The two of us had been good friends since we were 12, and my mom thought it was hysterical that I told her then I would marry him. She didn't take me seriously, but I was totally serious.

We had always promised each other we'd go to prom together, but when the time came, Andrew was dating a freshman girl and she wouldn't let him go with me. When I heard she was causing an issue, I found out she was in detention, and I stormed into the principal's office. I threatened to beat the shit out of her right in front of the principal. My mom had to come get me at school! Even though I had driven myself there, I had to be escorted out of the building and to my car. They were afraid I would jump the poor girl when she left. I got suspended for threatening her. That was the only time I had ever been suspended. Andrew ended up not going with me, and I gave him shit for years afterward for not taking me to prom.

Something was different that day at the beach. We were looking at each other . . . differently. Deep down I had always loved him more than as just a friend, but our relationship never went further when we were in school. That night he came back to my house and we kissed for the first time. The swarm of butterflies wildly fluttered in my stomach. I couldn't believe it was actually happening, that we were moving away from friendship status and into something more. I had been waiting for that moment for so long.

Over the next few weeks, we were together all the time and I was smitten. I had never loved anybody like Andrew, and instantly I was *in* love with him. I had always cared about guys I dated, but I never, ever felt this way about them. Things didn't stay blissful between us for long, though.

Fairly quickly, I noticed Andrew was drinking all the time. It didn't seem normal, but he was functioning fine, so it didn't seem like too much of an issue. He would start drinking early in the morning. At first I thought we were just having fun, but it was a problem. I had an inkling that he was also taking pills, but I never saw him do so. Sometimes we would go out to dinner and he'd be falling asleep at the table. Deep down I knew something was wrong.

The reality was, every time he hugged me and we kissed, I forgot about his bad habits. I loved being wrapped in his arms and still couldn't believe I was dating the guy I'd always known I would end up with. Andrew would sleep at my house a few nights a week and would wake up and leave before 8 a.m. I thought this was weird since he wasn't working, but he'd tell me he was heading home to shower and get ready for the day. He was always an early morning kind of guy, so I didn't think too much of it.

A few months into our relationship while I was at work, Andrew called me to ask if I could come home early. I could tell by his tone that something was wrong.

"I'll be home in an hour. What's going on?"

He was silent for a while. "Hil, I'm sick. I want you to come home now."

Sick? Like a cold? Take some medicine. Why are men so dramatic? I thought. I got home a little while later, and as soon as I saw him, I knew something wasn't right. He was sweaty and shaking. He told me we had to talk but was nervous to get the words out. He stumbled for a few minutes. His thoughts were all over the place, and I could tell he was skating around whatever it was he had to come clean about. He was pacing back and forth in my small bedroom not making eye contact with me. *This doesn't look like a cold. . . .*

"Andrew, what is going on? What's wrong? Just tell me already!"

He finally looked at me with eyes full of humiliation and dread.

"Hil, I need to self-detox. I am in a bad place. I've been using heroin, and it's gotten out of control. I'm so sorry."

I gazed at him blankly. *Did those words really just come out of his mouth?*

I tried to process what he had just said, but my brain wasn't understanding the information it was getting. My heart started pounding as the reality of the situation began to overcome my body and my mind. For one of the first times in my life, I was speechless. A few moments of awkward silence passed.

"HEROIN?!" *Are you fucking kidding me?*

I knew Andrew was drinking a lot and I had a hunch he was taking pills, but I had never imagined he was shooting heroin into his veins. He explained to me that his problem had started with pills, but since oxycodone and other opiates were too expensive in pill form, he started using intravenous heroin, which was much cheaper. Once he made that decision, there was no turning back.

I learned that Andrew was not leaving my house early to go home and shower; he was leaving my house at 8 a.m. to go shoot up. He couldn't start his day and deal with the anxieties of life, or love me, before the heroin entered his body. He wasn't falling asleep at dinner; he was nodding out from coming down off the dope. I started crying uncontrollably.

At this moment, I had absolutely *no* idea what I was in for. I obviously knew heroin was very bad and serious, but until you love someone who's a heroin addict, you really don't know *how* bad it is.

This was another "haze of after" moment, and the next chapter of my life would be centered around his addiction. My life would be forever changed.

September 21, 2010:

    I realized that everything I was trying not to believe, was actually true. For the past month or so I had noticed a change in Andrew and was questioning if he was doing drugs, but the sad reality is I love him and didn't want to believe anything, so all it took was for him to say no, and that was that. I have never been that girl, the one that I would talk about and say, "She's so stupid, how does she not see what he's doing? I can't believe she's still with him. . . ." Well, now I know, because I was that girl. I made excuses for Andrew to make myself feel better, and I pretended things were okay when they weren't. The past week or so we were fighting like crazy because I kept catching him in lies. I wasn't even trying to—what he was saying was legitimately not making sense.

Andrew told me he wanted to get off the drugs and was going to self-detox. At the time, I truly thought we would be able to spend the weekend dealing with this and then it'd be over. I was so naïve and had no idea what being a heroin addict even meant. I didn't know that this was the start of years of chaos and uncertainty.

Trying to remain supportive although I was unsure of what I was really getting into, I went with him while he picked up Xanax and Suboxone. Xanax would calm him down, and Suboxone is a drug used to help people get off opiates because it blocks the opiate's effects. It was so strong, though, that some people actually went to rehab to get off Suboxone.

My mom and Brock were up at Steven's parents' house for the weekend. For two days Andrew tried to self-detox in my room. We cried a lot. I was disappointed and couldn't believe my love story was turning out like this. I loved him so much so fast. I stayed up next to him while he slept to make sure he didn't have a seizure from withdrawal, which I had read online could happen.

A few days later his mom came home from a weekend away and we went to her house to tell her the truth. Andrew told her the situation, and she, like me, had known something was wrong but also had turned a blind eye—not believing it because we didn't want to believe it. We all agreed we were going to get him set up at a rehab, since self-detoxing from heroin in my bedroom was not proving to be successful.

Andrew and I went into his room and I asked him if there were drugs there. He said, "There's no heroin, but there is a lot of shit in here." I got a garbage bag and told him to sit down. I went drawer by drawer, eventually filling up the bag with things I had never seen in real life before. Syringes, pills, glass vials full of morphine. I opened one drawer and there was a beat-up belt. I knew it was what he used to tighten around his veins. I started bawling my eyes out. Andrew cried too. I felt like I was going to throw up.

After this traumatic cleanup, we sat with his mom and researched rehabs. We found a place in Brooklyn, but Andrew told us most of his dope dealers were there, so we decided to stay away from that one. Eventually we found a location out east in Suffolk County. I'll call it LICR. I called them, and a friendly man picked up.

"Hi, this is Joe. How can I help you?"

"Hi, Joe, my name is Hilary, and I need your help. My boyfriend is withdrawing from heroin and needs to be admitted somewhere immediately."

I could *not* believe the words coming out of my mouth. After a short talk, Andrew and Joe set up his intake for the next morning and that was that. In the space of four months I had graduated from college, fallen in love with the man I'd always wanted to be with, and set him up at rehab for a heroin addiction.

When it was time to say goodbye, we cried and Andrew told me he loved me more than anything. He thanked me for sticking by him and helping him. I hugged him tightly. It was hard to let go.

The next morning, I woke up to a blocked number calling me. Andrew was cheery on the other side. "Morning, babe!" He was clean for 24 hours and already sounded different. He told me that the place encouraged visitors and I could go see him the following week once his detox was over.

The day came and I drove the hour ride to see him, unsure of what I was about to walk into. The rehab had family members sit through an orientation before seeing our loved ones. They explained to us how the 12-Step program worked. They also told us that no matter how long our friends or family members remained clean, they would always be addicts. This did not sit well with me and made zero sense. The Andrew I fell in love with at 12 years old was not an addict, so why would he *always* be one? I trusted the professionals and listened, but deep down, I felt like they were wrong. They encouraged me to start attending Al-Anon and Nar-Anon meetings, which were like AA and NA meetings, but geared toward the addict's family members.

Finally, when I saw Andrew, he held me close. He looked good and seemed optimistic. We weren't allowed to be physical, but we hugged and snuck in a few kisses. I was happy to be back in his arms. My heart really believed that in 28 days, he'd be home and over this and we would move on.

I brought him some gifts, one of them being a bookmark that said, "Persistence: Rest When Tired, Just Don't Quit." Andrew didn't read much back then, but I liked the message. He loved it too. When he got home from rehab, he got the words "Rest when tired" tattooed on his right lower bicep, and "Just don't quit" on his left. I told him if he ever went to use again, he'd have to shoot up while reading those words— and maybe then he wouldn't quit on himself or on his sobriety. I thought it would help keep him clean.

———

Although my mom supported me in sticking with Andrew, she also made her concerns very clear about the situation I was in. Of course, she was not thrilled her daughter was involved with a heroin addict, but she had known Andrew since he was a kid and knew he was a good person who came from a good family. A few days after I saw him at rehab, she told me she wanted to come with me to a Nar-Anon meeting.

September 25, 2010:

My mom introduced herself to the group and said that she was there because her daughter is dating an addict and she is scared. Then she started to cry. She said she is scared that she's going to see me get my heart broken. It was hard to see my mom cry and tell these strangers how she is afraid of me getting hurt. But, as much as I appreciate the concern, I'm 22 years old, and whether or not my heart is going to be broken, by Andrew or by anyone else, is out of her control. After she was done talking, I thought it was the perfect time for me to speak. I felt like we needed a therapist. I said that yes, I am dating an addict, who is in recovery right now. I said I'm doing my best to be supportive and strong through this whole thing, and I'm trying to follow the 12 Steps that they encourage, but it is very difficult for me to find the hope and faith that these groups teach about, when I have my mother, who is supposed to be my number one support system, pretty much telling me there is no light at the end of the tunnel. Instead, it almost seems like she is setting me up for a horror at the end. No matter how the tunnel ends, my mom does not know. Neither do I. I almost feel like she's trying to prepare me for what is going to happen when Andrew relapses, like it's a given. Even though the statistics are against me, I'd like to hope that he is strong enough for 28 days to be all he needs.

Like most times in my life, my mom was right. This was just the beginning of Andrew's road to recovery.

23

POST-REHAB, FIRST TIME

When Andrew's 28-day program ended, I was happy to pick him up and bring him home. Everyone told us, "Day 29 is the hardest, when you wake up and are not in the comfort of the rehab"—and they were right. The first week or two when Andrew was home, things were good, but they were definitely not "fixed."

I was constantly questioning him and what he was doing. If he told me he had to shower, I would stick my head in to make sure he was really in there. If he didn't answer the phone, I panicked and called back five times in a row. I was not ready to trust him again, and he was not ready to let me in the way I felt I needed. If he decided he wanted to skip an AA/NA meeting, we would fight about it. All in all, it was not the fairy-tale post-rehab I had innocently hoped for. We decided we needed to take a break, and for the first time in my life, my heart was broken.

December 2, 2010:

Andrew has been out of rehab for a month and a half, and we grew a lot as a couple, while at the same time realizing we both need a little more independence. I have never loved anyone as much as I love Andrew. I have never even come close to feeling the way I do about him. But sometimes I forget I am also dealing with

an addict, and even though he is the person I want to be with, he needs to get
better on his own and get his life back on track, on his own, in order for him to be
in a relationship. I've heard this a million times throughout my life: "Sometimes
when you love something, you gotta let it go, and if it's meant to be, it will come
back and find you." That statement never meant anything to me until I knew
what it was like to love something. And now it means even more to me when I
have to do one of the hardest things I've ever done, and that's walk away from the
person I don't want to walk away from. I haven't slept alone in a while, and it's
only been a few nights but it's already a little weird. Everything reminds me of
him, and it's making it hard not to think about him. I need to keep myself
occupied and do me for a little, do things that I enjoy for myself. I'm mad at
myself for not starting my book. Maybe I should start now.

While Andrew and I were broken up, I thought about him every
single day. We would talk on and off because I wanted to make sure he
was staying clean. As December progressed, I started to get upset that
I wouldn't be with him for New Year's Eve.

"Jen, you have to get me out of this country!" I dramatically said to
her one day.

"Hil, what do you mean out of the country?"

I told her we should go away for New Year's because I wanted to
be as far away from Andrew as possible so I didn't have to think about
him. We were making good money but were still broke 22-year-olds,
so all we could afford was Canada. We planned a five-day trip to
Montreal.

January 8, 2011:

I can't believe that it's 2011! Montreal was NUTS. It was awesome to go
away with my best friend, celebrate New Year's, and escape for a little bit. Jen
keeps telling me the world is going to end in 2012 and she's going to be pissed if I
don't get my book out before then. My New Year's resolution is to start
writing it.

It's crazy to read the last few entries and remember those days and those
feelings, what I was going through with Andrew . . . and to see where I am now. I
think looking back on the past few months I can see how I have personally

changed. It's not anything I can actually see, but I feel it. Being in love really tossed me around mentally, but in the end I know I grew from it. I learned, for one, what it was like to be loved. That in turn showed me what I deserve, because at a point, I stopped getting it from Andrew. The sad reality is that Andrew has nothing to give me right now. I love him very much and I know that he loves me, but we can't use that as the only reason to stay together. We both know what we went through this summer. Being with Andrew also showed me that I am capable of loving someone, really, deeply loving someone. . . . I wouldn't have gone through what I went through with him if I didn't love him. It showed me how strong I was and how weak I could be—how naïve I could be. On top of all this, I'm trying to deal with the fact that the first time I have ever been in love, I was lied to on a daily basis. When it was good it was great, and when it was bad it was terrible. No matter what, I'll always wish the best for him. I love him so much, it sucks.

Even though I didn't think Andrew had anything to give to me, by the following month, we were back together. We loved each other too much and too deeply not to be together. We tried our best to navigate through this process, and he agreed he would be more open with me to try to alleviate some of my trust issues.

This was only the beginning, and even then, I would have done anything for him.

24
ARREST #1

When Andrew and I got back together, we spent every day and every night together. I would take him to his AA/NA meetings and always thought I had my eye on him, making sure he stayed on the right track.

At the end of March, I told Sam I was going to take her to Atlantic City for her birthday. I was nervous to leave Andrew, but he told me he would be fine and encouraged me to have a good night away. He said I deserved it and assured me that everything would be okay.

I picked Sam up on March 29, 2011, and we drove to AC, ready for a fun night of gambling. I had been practically babysitting Andrew over the last two months and was looking forward to a night away.

We got to AC and immediately hit the blackjack table. We were having a blast. Within an hour of being there, my phone starting ringing from an unknown number. I ignored it. Immediately the number called back. I got up and answered.

"Hil, it's me, you have to come home," Andrew frantically blurted.

"What? What's wrong? What number is this?"

"Hil, I got arrested. I'm at the police station."

I could feel my blood start to boil.

"Are you fucking kidding me, Andrew? I leave you for *one* night and you get arrested? What happened?"

Andrew told me that he and his friend Corey were heading home from Brooklyn and got pulled over. Corey and Andrew were close friends and had been since before Andrew and I started dating. Corey was a year older than we were, but we all went to high school together and had known each other for a while. The three of us hung out often and had a lot of good, funny times. Corey was loved by everyone that knew him. I knew Corey was struggling with drugs also, but the two of them would go to AA/NA meetings together with Corey's dad, so I thought they were helping each other get through a similar situation.

As soon as I heard Andrew say "Brooklyn," I knew he was using again. A rush of doubt filled my body as I realized he must not have remained sober the last two months. Once again I'd been fooled. I was hurt and angry. I told him I was *not* coming home to rescue him and he had to deal with it himself. Obviously, I did not enjoy the remainder of my night. I couldn't believe that the *one* night I left Andrew in two months, he got arrested.

The next day I got home and drove to Andrew's house. He was remorseful, but I was enraged. I looked at his police report and became even more infuriated. Andrew was charged with criminal possession of a controlled substance in the seventh degree; possession of a hypodermic instrument; criminal possession of marijuana; unlawful possession of marijuana; possession of a controlled substance in a non-original container; operating a motor vehicle without a seat belt; and depositing refuse on the highway.

I read the charges a few times, trying to process how badly he had really screwed up.

"A hypodermic instrument? So, you relapsed?"

He looked at me regretfully and said he was sorry. I felt betrayed but hadn't even begun to fully understand how sick he really was.

Andrew's mom found a lawyer who said he would try to get Andrew transferred out of criminal court and into drug court. Drug court combined criminal justice with medical treatment, and after the defendant successfully completed a drug program, charges were typically reduced or dismissed—whereas in criminal court, he'd be facing punishment for the crimes. The arraignment was a few months away, so in the meantime, Andrew was told to be on his best behavior, to stay clean, and not to fuck up again.

I stuck by Andrew throughout this time. He started an outpatient program to show the court he was working to stay clean, and I tried to remain hopeful that he was on the road to recovery . . . again.

25

"BABY, IT'S OKAY, I'M OKAY"

A few weeks after the arrest, I was working a double shift and didn't get home on those nights until after 11 p.m. On the days I worked doubles I was always anxious, since Andrew was out of my supervision for so long. His mom was out of town, so we planned to stay at his house over the weekend to have some privacy. He knew I'd be over late and was texting me while I was at work that he was excited to have a weekend alone together. Even though I didn't fully trust him, he always gave me butterflies.

I called Andrew when I was leaving work to tell him I'd be there soon, but he didn't answer. I got to my mom's house and changed my clothes, called to tell him I'd be there in a minute, still no answer. I started to get worried.

I sped to Andrew's house and tried to open the front door, but it was locked. I was knocking and ringing the doorbell, but he wasn't answering. His car was in the driveway, so I thought he might be in the backyard.

I walked around the back—no Andrew in sight. I went to the back door and peered through the window.

I started to scream.

I saw one of the dining room chairs knocked over and Andrew

lying on the floor, motionless. The back door was unlocked, but my hands were shaking so bad I couldn't get it open. I was screaming through the window, "ANDREW, GET UP! GET UP!" while trying to get inside. I finally busted the back door open and ran over to him.

I started screaming louder.

There was foam pouring out of his mouth. I had only seen that in movies when someone was having a seizure. There was a syringe lying next to his lifeless body. The belt was still wrapped around his arm.

"ANDREW! WAKE UP! WAKE THE FUCK UP!" I was screaming while smacking him in the face.

He wasn't moving.

I ran to the kitchen and filled pitchers of cold water. I ran back to him. My entire body was shaking with adrenaline I had never felt before. I was pouring the water on his face, smacking him repeatedly, screaming and pleading for him to wake up. I tried to find a pulse but had no idea how, and with my shaky hands I couldn't feel anything but my body trembling.

"DO NOT DIE ON ME NOW! WAKE UP!"

I peeled his eyelids back. The whites of his beautiful bright blue eyes were yellow, like death was sinking in. I put my fingers under his nose but barely felt any air come out. I was crying and screaming, hitting him harder, pouring more buckets of water on him.

It seemed like hours passed, but I don't know how long it took, when unexpectedly Andrew slowly opened his eyes. He was extremely confused and didn't know where he was. I felt a sense of relief and started squeezing and hugging him while he was still on the floor. He was soaked, the foam and water still falling down his cheeks.

"Hil . . . I'm okay . . . I'm okay," he said slowly with one eye open.

Andrew tried to stand up, but he couldn't. His legs weren't working. It was like they were spaghetti. He would try to get up, but he'd fall. I was confused and scared. I tried to help him stand, but he'd fall again. I did not understand what was happening.

I started to panic, again. "Andrew, what is happening? STAND UP!"

He couldn't. His body was shutting down.

He sat back down on the soaked floor, defeated. His eyes were still yellow and lifeless. I got him water and a napkin. I wiped off his face and we sat on the floor together, taking deep breaths. Both of us were trying to calm down.

Some time passed and we tried to get him up again. He was finally able to stand. He was still confused and in a daze and said he wanted to take a shower. I sat on the toilet while he was in there, my face buried in my hands, crying hysterically the whole time.

He kept sticking his head out from the shower curtain. "Baby, it's okay, I'm okay."

He was not okay.

We got into bed and cried more. He held me tight and kept thanking me, which made me cry harder. I couldn't believe what had just happened.

Why didn't I call 911? Why didn't we go to the hospital when he couldn't stand? In my shock I couldn't think straight, and in the midst of trying to get him up, my 22-year-old self was afraid that 911 would get the cops involved, and I didn't want him to go to jail. Stupid. I risked his life to keep him out of jail. I don't know why I went for the cold water, or why it worked, but we were lucky it did.

I soon found out that it's pretty easy to remain on drugs during outpatient treatment, since heroin and other opiates only stay in your system for about three days. Andrew had a routine: after he would pass a drug test, he'd immediately go out and get high, knowing he had about a week to flush the drugs out of his body before the next test.

Sometimes I ask myself, what would have happened if I hadn't gotten to his house when I did? How long was he lying there? What if I had stopped for gas, or gotten stuck later at work? What if the back door had been locked? Would I have watched him die, right there on his living room floor, with me watching through the window? Would he have died alone, with a syringe and belt as the only things surrounding him?

Did I really save his life?

26

ARREST #2

I never told a single soul about the overdose. I was embarrassed for staying with Andrew, ashamed that he wasn't getting better, and scared of what was to come. To think back, I can't believe that was only the beginning.

Some people might think I should have broken up with him after something like this, but the overdose made me want to be with him more, as messed up as that sounds. *If I leave him, he will die. If I leave him, who will be there to save him?* As a psychology student who earned an A+ in a class called Addictive and Compulsive Behaviors, I knew I was the textbook definition of codependency. The truth is, though, it is much easier to read and learn about addiction than it is to love someone with an addiction.

A month later Andrew and I were somewhat back on track. However, that night replayed in my head over and over again. The trauma of finding him the way I did could not escape my mind. The feeling I experienced when I saw him was something I couldn't move on from. The pure panic and horror of thinking he was dead. At any given moment I would randomly start crying, recalling how he looked with foam streaming out of his mouth. The thought of a needle and belt would nauseate me. I'd get physically sick when I had to have blood drawn at the doctor. To this day, whenever I see a needle, the first thing I think of is heroin.

I wanted so badly for Andrew to get better but didn't know how to help, other than just to be there for him. *He's already in treatment; what more can I do?*

One night I was back at work, working the double again, and Andrew came to hang out with me. His friend dropped him off since Andrew had his car taken away after he got arrested. He was hanging at the bar with me and had a few drinks. I know this sounds crazy, but I can't pretend I was perfect. I was literally the one serving him the drinks like a fucking idiot. He had overdosed a month ago, was in drug treatment, and here I am serving him alcohol, while at the same time I think I'm being the world's best, most supportive girlfriend. Since I had seen the heroin practically kill him, I thought that was the bigger problem. They both were, but that is the truth as to how I felt.

I was lost. I didn't know how to love him without enabling him.

Andrew asked if he could take my car back to town and said he'd come back to pick me up when I was done with work. I handed him the keys. Ten minutes later my phone started ringing. It was Andrew. He was panicking.

"Hil, I got into an accident, I crashed into the guardrail, and your car is really fucked up. You have to come here right now."

I thought we were already at rock bottom and could not believe things were getting worse. I called Sam and she came and picked me up. We got to the accident site and Andrew was sitting on the side of the road in my totaled car. He'd had a lot more drinks than I knew, and he was on pills. I could never tell when Andrew was drunk because he barely got drunk—his tolerance was so high. Not to say I wasn't at fault, but I wouldn't have lent him my car if I'd known he had eight drinks. I had only served him two or three. Ever since Jonny's accident I was very careful about drinking and driving. I thought we had all learned that lesson.

I made Andrew call the police, yes, on himself. I told Sam to leave and I called my mom, who frantically drove to meet me at the accident site. We watched the police give Andrew a sobriety test, which he failed miserably. He was put in handcuffs and I sat on the side of the road, crying as they drove him away. Andrew was looking at me through the back window of the police car.

My mom peered at me, disappointed in him and sad for me. She didn't say much. Her silence killed me because I knew what she was thinking. We waited for the tow truck and she took me home. A few hours later Andrew called and said he was being released. He asked if I could get him. Somehow my mom agreed to let me borrow her car, since mine was in pieces. Of course, I went to pick him up.

The next day my mom sat us down and essentially told us we had to get our shit together. She gave us a lecture that we deserved. She was frustrated I was in a relationship like this since all the bad things going on were a direct result of Andrew's life and addictions. I was just bearing the consequences. She knew there was nothing she could say to get me to leave him, but she let us know how disappointed she was. Then we went to his mom's house to tell her about this arrest. We also called his lawyer.

The lawyer basically said that the situation was as bad as we had imagined. He encouraged Andrew to go back to rehab. Now he had all the drug charges pending from the first arrest plus all the charges from the accident.

His second set of charges were criminal possession of a controlled substance; operating a motor vehicle with 0.08 percent or more of alcohol in blood; operating a motor vehicle while intoxicated; unlawful possession of marijuana; speeding at a rate not reasonable and prudent; and possession of an open alcoholic beverage in a motor vehicle container.

The whole situation was a fucking nightmare. Andrew did not want to go back to rehab, but his lawyer said that it would look good to the court if he willingly checked himself in. The attorney explained that after having two drug-and-alcohol-related arrests within three months of each other, going to rehab would at least make it look like Andrew was trying to get himself help.

Like the first time, we called LICR to get Andrew enrolled. I was hesitant to use that rehab again because clearly it did not work the first time. But it was what we knew, so we did it. Within a few days, Andrew was back at rehab. I was crushed that he was gone again but relieved he was getting help. I tried to stay optimistic. *Maybe this time he'll get better.* I continued to visit him regularly and tried to be his rock.

Two weeks into his stay, Andrew called me to check in. We were catching up and he said, "Babe, you are never going to believe who showed up today."

"You mean like a celebrity?" I asked.

"No. Corey is here."

My heart sank. I loved Corey as a person, but the two of them were not good for each other at that time in their lives. This was the same Corey who got arrested with Andrew the night I went to Atlantic City. Andrew and Corey were very similar. They were both *way* too smart for their own good. Deep down they both had hearts of gold. Their friendship was built around the fact that they were similarly lost. I was incredibly uneasy that Corey was there; I thought it would take away Andrew's focus.

Andrew assured me that everything would be fine and that it was nice to have a familiar face around. Since they were both facing some of the same charges, Corey had decided to go to rehab for the same reason Andrew's lawyer had advised him to go: to look better to the courts come arraignment day.

At the end of Andrew's 28-day program, I drove out to the rehab to pick him up. When I walked in the front door, Corey was waiting there with him. I was confused, knowing Corey's program was not over yet.

"Hey, Hil, I'm ready to go home. Do you mind if I get a ride back to town with you?" Corey asked.

Since they were not mandated to be there, the truth was they could leave whenever they wanted. I wasn't going to leave Corey stranded, so I asked him if he was sure he wanted to leave, and he said yes. We packed up the car and headed back to town.

This time around, Andrew's mom said he was not welcome back at her house. She was using a tough-love approach, and no one could blame her. But of course, Andrew needed a place to go. I begged and begged my mom, and somehow she agreed to let Andrew come back and live with us. When we got there my mom laid out the rules: no drugs, no drinking, or he was out.

Obviously I was nervous that Andrew was home, but every time he held me, my heart melted. I loved him deeply, even though some nights with him were the hardest moments of my life.

———

Andrew's arraignment date was set for a few weeks after he came home. Corey was being arraigned on the same day, so we met him at the courthouse. We nervously waited for the judge to call Andrew's name, and when he did, Andrew's lawyer accompanied him to the front of the room.

Andrew's lawyer showed the judge paperwork from the completed drug treatment program and said Andrew was on the road to recovery. The courts agreed to move Andrew's case to drug court, but he had to plead guilty to the DWI charge. Andrew lost his driver's license, was put on probation for three years, and had to pay a few hundred dollars in fines. We left the courtroom relieved he wasn't going to jail. We sat outside and waited for Corey.

Some time passed and Corey never came out. We poked our heads back into the courtroom and he wasn't there. His public defender told us that Corey had some prior charges and the judge had set bail, but his parents wouldn't pay it. They were trying the same tough-love approach as Andrew's mom, so we couldn't blame them either. We did not have the money to bail Corey out, so unfortunately we had to leave him there. Corey was kept in county jail and then went straight to a sober home.

———

A couple of weeks later, Jen and I were at work and her mom called us, panicking. "Girls, I'm so sorry, please sit down. I have to tell you something. . . ."

We knew someone had died. We had gotten these calls too many times before.

"Mom, who is it? What happened?" Jen said frantically.

"Corey passed away last night."

I stopped in my tracks, startled and saddened by the news. Jen and Corey had been friends for years. They were in the same grade, and since her mom was like family to me, she knew about Corey and Andrew's friendship and history. I ran out of work to head home to make sure I was the one who told Andrew his closest friend had died. Even though their friendship was based on drugs, they truly did love each other and had gone through some serious shit together.

I sped home and ran upstairs. Andrew was still sleeping. I shook him and woke him up, telling him he needed to get out of bed.

"What the hell, Hil, what's wrong? Why are you home?"

"Babe, I am so sorry to tell you this. . . . Corey died last night."

Andrew jolted up and looked at me blankly. He was quiet for a while. "He killed himself?"

I was extremely confused by this question. I actually did not know how Corey had died, but I assumed he'd overdosed.

"Umm, I don't think so. I think he overdosed, honey. I am so, so sorry."

"No. He didn't," Andrew said, sure of himself and annoyed at my assumption. He got up and put his clothes on. He told me he was going to see Corey's parents and ran out of the house in a hurry.

A few days later, we went to Corey's wake. I couldn't believe the last time I saw him was in court. I felt like a really shitty person. I felt guilty that I had driven him home early from rehab, that maybe if I'd told him no, he would have finished the program and this could have had a different ending.

I was looking around at everyone crying. *Holy shit. This could be Andrew.* I was looking at Corey's parents. They reminded me of

Jonny's parents. There was nothing anyone could do to take their pain away. Corey's dad hugged Andrew and said, "You better stay on the right path." They cried together. It was hard to watch.

We found out at the wake that Corey had committed suicide. Andrew somehow knew that he hadn't overdosed. When I asked Andrew how he knew, he said, "Corey and I spoke about this before. We didn't know how to get out of our situations." It ripped my heart apart to know they both had talked about taking their lives.

The world truly lost a beautiful soul. Corey was funny, outgoing, incredibly smart, and always a pleasure to be around. He was lost, just like Andrew was. He did not deserve to die.

I tried to find comfort in knowing that Jonny and Corey had been friends when they were both alive. I told myself they were in heaven together watching over all of us.

Rest in Peace
12/09/1986–09/22/2011

27

THE WORST OF TIMES WAS YET TO COME

After Corey died, Andrew started using and drinking again. I knew it, and again, I turned a blind eye. Andrew's addictions got so bad that sometimes I honestly did not know *how* I still loved him. But I did. I loved him so much.

Andrew wasn't using because of anything that had to do with me. He was broken inside, but I would always question myself: *Why am I not enough? Why isn't this relationship enough?* When you are dating an addict, their drug use has nothing to do with you, and that is incredibly hard to accept when you are doing everything for them.

In 2012 we moved out of my mom's house and got an apartment together. We also decided to add a beautiful pit bull puppy, Cayman, to our family. Part of me thought having our own place and adding a dog to our relationship would persuade Andrew to change, as silly as that sounds. Spoiler alert: it didn't. When we picked up Cayman, though, we had great times. I loved seeing Andrew train her and snuggle with her. She brought us joy during a dark period.

It's hard to imagine that the worst of times was yet to come. From then through 2014, it was a drug and alcohol free-for-all. Andrew was drinking a 12-pack of beer before lunchtime, he was shooting heroin as often as 10 times a day, and he was taking pills, mainly oxycodone and other opiates, sometimes crushing them and shooting them or smoking them. He freebased fentanyl patches a few times. If the veins in his arms and legs were too depleted, he'd shoot up in his foot.

Seeing Andrew on pills always made me feel like extra shit about myself. When I was selling pills in high school, I did it with zero consideration for who or what the pills were going toward. What if I sold someone Xanax and they got into a car accident and hurt themselves or someone else? It wasn't until I saw Andrew's addiction and how much it affected my life that I realized just how irresponsible and thoughtless my actions had been.

Andrew was going to outpatient drug rehab and seeing a drug counselor because he was mandated to by the court. As in the past, he would stay clean for a few days, pass the drug test, and then use that night. As far as the court knew, with all his clean tests and rehab work, he was improving. Yeah, right.

Andrew was always one of the smartest people in a room. He was incredibly bright. It was frustrating that he was so smart but acting so fucking stupid. I constantly reminded myself how in high school, we were the ones in honors and AP classes together. I would take myself back to when we were 16, the mornings when my mom would drop me off at his house at 7 a.m. since we both had off first period, and he'd cook me breakfast in his underwear. Those were the moments I fell in love with him, and those were the moments I tried to remember.

Throughout this time, I noticed myself starting to change, and not for the better. I was no angel during this period of our lives. I was drinking more often than normal. Sometimes to escape, sometimes to try and get near his level. Andrew and I would fight all the time. Our fights would get physical. I would become so angry with him after catching him in a lie or finding drugs, I would push and hit him. He never hit me back, but he would shove me to get me off him, which would infuriate me and I'd come back swinging. I was snapping like a light switch, just like my dad did when I was growing up.

One horrible New Year's Eve, Andrew and I got into a blowout argument after a night full of too much alcohol. To be spiteful, he called a dope dealer right in front of me. Even when I was drunk and incoherent, I always knew Andrew was one bad needle away from dying. My desperation in these times, mixed with alcohol, resulted in rageful anger. I went crazy hitting him and yelling. He walked out of the room, and that's when I spotted his wallet on the table. I hid it.

When the dealer showed up, Andrew was tearing apart our tiny apartment looking everywhere for his wallet. I watched with a smirk on my face, almost impressed by how focused he was. I saw the dealer waiting in the street and walked outside. As I crossed the lawn and stormed toward his car, I was screaming that I was taking his license plate number and reporting him to the cops for murdering people with his drugs. Andrew came chasing after me shouting to get back inside, and he fell down eight stairs on the way. The dealer sped away yelling back at me that I was "fucking crazy." When we got inside, the fighting continued for a while. Andrew slept on the couch that night, but I was in bed with a smile on my face. The night was a shitshow, but he didn't shoot heroin—so I considered that a win.

One night we were in Atlantic City and fought so bad, we shoved each other so hard into the toilet that the tank exploded, cracked, and water started pouring out. We left AC at three o'clock in the morning while the bathroom was flooding. We screamed at each other and fought the entire three-hour ride. Andrew drove home and hit 130-plus mph in his car that night. We were reckless, and in a dangerous, horrible place.

At all times throughout these three years, we were at an intensity level of 100, from the moment we woke up to the moment we went to sleep. Our relationship was full of traumatic, deep, serious situations, all mixed up with our intense love, friendship, and desire, and it was all overshadowed by sadness, mistrust, and addiction.

It was a cocktail of disaster.

Of course, there were good times. And when they came around, we chose to ignore everything else. Those moments were what I held on to during the bad times. When I was in his arms, it was just him and me. When I wasn't, it was him and his drugs. I always knew that the man I loved was somewhere deep inside of him, but I was getting tired of waiting for that man to emerge.

For years I had been lying to my friends, my family, and everyone else I knew. I stopped hanging out with my friends, because I was lying so much, it was easier to just stay home. Andrew's addiction was *way* worse than anybody knew and I was humiliated and embarrassed, so I became a recluse. I stopped writing in my diary since I didn't want to lie in there and I knew I would. It was exhausting.

Throughout these years, I was having recurring dreams of my teeth falling out. I would be standing over a sink and all my teeth would be cracking and breaking in pieces as they came out of my mouth. I'd wake up soaked in sweat with my heart pounding, immediately grabbing my teeth to make sure everything was in place. I looked up the meaning: teeth falling out is symbolic of personal loss, anxiety, depression, instability, insecurity, jealousy, and going through "more stress than normal." *No shit.*

I had this dream every few weeks for years, until Andrew turned his life around.

28

I CAN'T BELIEVE THAT GIRL IS ME

There were nights when Andrew and I would agree to have a night alone and stay in but then he'd change his mind and say he wanted to go out. Trying to be tough and stick my ground, I would stay home by myself, silently protesting his behavior. He would go out to party with our friends. The problem with dating someone in your group of friends is, when shit hits the fan, people have to choose a side. With Andrew, a lot of times our friends chose him, especially since I would be sitting at home alone. The truth is, they had *no idea* what we were going through. Since I had been lying to them about everything being fine, I came off as the "controlling bitchy girlfriend." It wasn't like Andrew was shooting heroin in front of them, so they just thought he was drinking too much, but they didn't have to deal with the reality.

One night Andrew and I were hanging out when all of a sudden his behavior changed. I knew what that meant. He wanted to use. Once the thought of using was implanted in his mind, there was nothing anyone could do to stop him. He could not overcome his impulses to get high. He started fighting with me that he needed to leave, but since he had no car, he needed me to drive him.

"Are you kidding me? I am not taking you anywhere!"

Andrew was charming and manipulative. He was the ultimate

addict. He knew how to get people to do things for him to benefit himself and his addiction. I was his prime target.

After going back and forth for an hour, he somehow convinced me that if I took him this *one* time, he would come clean to me about everything he had done in the past. He promised me that he would truthfully answer any questions I had and he would "never use again."

The definition of codependency is "excessive emotional or psychological reliance on a partner, typically one who requires support on account of an illness or addiction." They might as well have put my picture in the dictionary—this was me to a tee. Somehow, as crazy as this may sound, I truly believed in that moment that by taking Andrew to pick up heroin, I would somehow be in control of the situation and get all the answers I had wanted for so long.

I reluctantly got in my car, and he told me where to go. My heart was pounding. *What am I doing? Am I crazy?*

I was crazy.

The reality was, with or without me, Andrew would have found a way to get his drugs. I knew if I stayed home he would go out and get high anyway. This had happened so many times before, and I was always left alone in my room, worried and anxious. When he'd leave, I felt like I couldn't control what was happening, and of course, I could not. In this moment, I really thought I could get control over the situation. Of course, I couldn't.

I drove Andrew to a gas station where he got out, picked up the dope, and got back in my car. The time he overdosed, I found him close to death. Now I was driving him to get the same drug that had nearly killed him. At times I hated the person I was becoming. *What the fuck is wrong with me?*

My heart was racing. Andrew looked at me, almost as if he felt sorry for what he was about to do, but he didn't say a word. I started to cry. I knew what was about to happen.

As I drove home with tears streaming down my face, Andrew shot up in the passenger seat next to me, using the seat belt to tighten around his arm. I felt like I knew where the heroin was in his veins. It was like I could see through him as each muscle began to relax one by one. The drug took over his body and he was immediately at ease.

I stared ahead, driving, crying. I couldn't believe what I had just done. I couldn't believe how quickly the drugs affected him. Part of me was curious to know what he was feeling. What 15-second rush would cause someone to sacrifice all their relationships and life goals? Part of me wanted to know what it felt like. But as stupid as I was acting, luckily I wasn't stupid enough to cross that line.

Let me clarify that to this day, this was one of the worst and hardest moments of my entire life. I was so naïve, so stupid to think that I was making the situation safer. What could I have done if he had overdosed right there in my car? Nothing. I was young and senseless. I was enabling to a level I couldn't comprehend at the time. It was traumatic to have him get high six inches away from me. Something I had fought against for years, I allowed to happen in my car.

Looking back, I think part of me was afraid that it was only a matter of time until he overdosed again. When it first happened, I arrived at his house in time to find him and save him. My fear was that the next time, he'd be alone and would die. Maybe I thought by bringing him to pick up the drugs, I could at least monitor the situation. The truth is, to this day, flashbacks of that night pop into my mind and I get sick to my stomach. I see what happened from the vantage point of someone staring into my car through my windshield. I see it from another point of view. Watching these two poor souls, in love and lost, trying to navigate a fucked-up situation.

I can't believe that girl is me.

29

JUST WHEN I THOUGHT WE WERE AT OUR LOWEST POINT, IT GOT LOWER

As the years went on, I found myself acting like a private detective. Of course after the gas station night, Andrew was still using, even though he'd told me he would "never use again." I was an idiot to believe him. I loved him so much, every minute of every day, but all the love in the world was not enough for him to change. Andrew would be at work and I would rummage through the house, looking for drugs and paraphernalia. I'd find syringes hidden in sneakers, jacket pockets, notebooks, under sinks. I'd spread them out on a table waiting for Andrew to come home so I could confront him and fight with him. I would hit him and go crazy. It was a shitshow.

Andrew would tell me he'd stopped drinking and I'd come home to find him passed out on the couch with an empty 12-pack next to him. Sometimes I'd come home and know he was high from the moment I saw him. His pin-sized pupils told me all the truth I needed. He was a functioning addict who covered it up in public, but deep down, I always knew when he was lying.

I'd wake up in the mornings to the sound of him throwing up. For months, he was throwing up every single day. We didn't tell anyone. His body was rejecting all the alcohol he was filling it with. The daily combination of alcohol, heroin, and pills was causing his body to revolt against him, but Andrew wasn't listening. His body was trying to tell us something was wrong—something was very wrong.

In the back of my head I knew he could die any day. At night, I'd wake up to Andrew moaning loudly. At his worst, he was shooting heroin 10 times a day. When he would sleep, his body would go through withdrawal from being without the dope for so many hours. The pain of his nightly mini-withdrawals caused the moaning—it sounded horrific. Our friends were dying, opiates were taking over our town, and every few months we'd hear of people we knew—or didn't know—who were overdosing and dying. I knew Andrew was going to die.

We moved from one apartment to another, and I was so happy to have our puppy with me. When Andrew would leave me to go out to party, I would sit and snuggle Cayman and cry. She would lick away my tears, and I'd feel like I wasn't so alone. I'd tell her "Daddy is being a real piece of shit" and vent to her. She was the only "person" I didn't have to lie to.

At the time, I was leading a double life. By now, I had gotten a job through one of my VIP customers at the OTB. He told me I was too smart to be serving him gin and tonics all night and offered me a job at his company. I didn't know anything about his business or what it was, but I was ready to move on from waitressing. He hired me, and within three months I got a $10,000 raise and a big promotion. I always excelled in learning new things and yearned to be successful. I would go to work and people would call me a "rock star." Then I'd come home and battle Andrew's addictions, night after night, and no one had any clue.

———

One day, "Christine," a close girlfriend of mine, told me she was going to come over to see our new apartment. I told Andrew, and he was not thrilled at all. When she arrived at the house, she called and asked me to come outside. When I got to her car, she told me to hop in. She drove around the corner, parked, and said we needed to talk.

Christine proceeded to tell me that a few weeks prior, when my friends were all at a party, she had slept with Andrew.

"Ummmm, what??"

She told me how sorry she was and that they had both been really drunk and it meant nothing, but that she couldn't hide it from me any longer. As if this wasn't messed up enough, the night they slept together was one of those nights that I tried to stand my ground and stay home while Andrew decided at the last minute he wanted to go out. I had texted Christine after he left and asked her to keep an eye on him. She was texting me all night giving me updates and telling me what he was doing. She forgot to include that she had sex with him.

Christine had been one of my closest friends since high school, and to this day I give her kudos for having the balls to drive to my house and tell me this face-to-face, especially since Andrew was cowardly hiding it from me. I told her to drive me home. I was angry but too shocked to react.

When I got back upstairs, Andrew was pacing around the apartment—he knew she had told me. The second I saw him I fucking lost it. I was throwing things, knocking over chairs, screaming at him and smacking him.

"You want to shoot up heroin and mess yourself up? FINE. But you slept with one of my friends, you dirty piece of shit?" I roared.

The reality of the news started to sink in, and with it came soul-shattering devastation. I had done everything for Andrew. I was so loyal. I stuck by him through the worst of times. And he cheated on me. I could not believe it.

Andrew was crying and kept telling me how sorry he was, how drunk he was that night, and how he didn't care about Christine and it meant nothing—all the things that people tell their girlfriends after they get caught cheating. We were living together and neither of us had anywhere else to go. Andrew slept on the couch for a while, and it was a really rough time for us, for me specifically.

I soon learned that most of my friends knew about what happened and they all had hidden it from me. I was crushed. Once again I was humiliated and embarrassed by our relationship. I felt sad, dirty, angry, and alone. I couldn't believe that I had seen my friends a few times since that night and nobody had told me. *How could they look me in the eyes and not tell me?* I knew Andrew was the one at fault, but I was beyond hurt by my friends.

I can see how it could be perceived as hypocritical that I stayed with Andrew but ended my friendship with Christine. The truth was, I knew that Andrew was more broken than anyone realized. I knew he didn't care about Christine and that he truly did love me, but I felt so dumb for staying with him. I knew I deserved better. I tried to forgive Christine, but I couldn't get myself to ever look at her again. We have not spoken since that night in her car. This also ended my relationships with a few other longtime girlfriends, and I don't blame them for staying friends with Christine. It was hard for anyone to remain friends with both of us, and I was so secretive about what Andrew and I were dealing with, I understand that people had to make a choice, and that choice was not me.

It took me a long time to be able to look at and speak to Andrew without going crazy. I didn't have sex with him for months. Doing drugs and drinking was something he did that hurt himself—of course it hurt me too—but he was doing it to himself. Cheating on me, after all that I had been through with him, was heartbreaking and defeating.

Just when I thought we were at our lowest point, it got lower.

30

A FUNERAL OR A WEDDING

After Andrew cheated on me, I became even more of a recluse. I was really fucked up in the head over this. I would go to work and not speak to anyone. Some of my coworkers would ask me what was wrong and I would just start to cry. I was embarrassed and angry beyond comprehension. I didn't know why I was staying with Andrew. Sometimes I considered myself a "ride-or-die girlfriend" because I was sticking by the person I loved through the good and the bad. Other times I thought I was pathetic. *How can I still love him as much as I do? What is wrong with me? Why can't I leave him?*

Again, I held on to the fact that I knew who Andrew really was from our childhood. I knew how amazing he was underneath the addict, and I know it seems stupid for me to say this, but I really did know how much he loved me, despite the fact that the things he was doing were not what you do to someone you love.

In June of 2014, I was at work one day when Andrew texted me that he wasn't feeling well. I got home that night, walked into the house, and he was white as a ghost. He was drenched with sweat, literally dripping off his ears and nose.

I thought he was dope sick, so I became angry. Andrew insisted he wasn't and that something serious was happening. He said he had excruciating pains in his stomach and he was having a hard time taking deep breaths. It was hard for me to be sympathetic since I was still fuming about him cheating, but I took him to the doctor because something didn't seem right. We went to a walk-in clinic around the corner, and they told us they thought he had appendicitis. They sent us home and said if it got worse to go to the hospital, but meanwhile, they set us up for an MRI/CT scan appointment the following morning.

That night Andrew was incredibly sick. It was like he had a horrible version of the flu. He was throwing up, had a fever, had no color in his body, and couldn't stop sweating. I've never seen anyone sweat that much. The next morning we got to his appointment, and as soon as the technician laid eyes on him she told us something was very wrong. While Andrew went into the room, I stayed outside. A few minutes later another technician came out and told me that Andrew's veins were so depleted they couldn't get an IV in to give him fluids to try to stabilize him. They knew his veins were destroyed from heroin.

The technician took me to a private room. "Honey, you know he is very sick, right? He needs serious help."

I looked at her and nodded. *Yeah, lady, trust me, I know.*

A short while later, a few more technicians came out and told us that Andrew had a serious case of acute pancreatitis and we needed to go straight to the hospital. They told us they had already called the ER, which happened to be across the street, and a nurse would be waiting to speed him through triage. Everything happened so fast, and they seemed very serious. We knew something bad was happening.

Andrew and I were both confused. We didn't know what pancreatitis was, but it was obvious that he was sick. He still had no color in his face and was sweating profusely. We drove across the street and, just like they said, a nurse was waiting.

"Are you Andrew?" she asked.

They took us right in. *That was weird—I never saw a nurse waiting for someone to arrive at an ER like that. . . .*

Andrew was immediately admitted to the intensive care unit, and the doctors asked me who his next of kin was. This was becoming way too serious for me to handle alone, so I called his mom, who was at her Massachusetts house at the time. I told her what was happening and she got in the car to meet me as quickly as she could.

Shortly after Andrew was put in a room, a doctor came in to confirm that he did have acute pancreatitis and they knew it was caused by his severe alcoholism. We learned that his daily puking sessions leading up to this were his body trying to alert us that he was poisoning himself—over and over again.

The doctor looked at Andrew. "You are 26 years old and you have the liver of a 50-year-old alcoholic. You can never drink alcohol again, or you are going to die."

This was crazy for me to hear. I knew Andrew was an addict and an alcoholic, but I never thought about the permanent damage he was doing to his body and his organs. The doctors started treating Andrew immediately. His pancreas was full of pseudocysts (collections of leaked pancreatic fluids), which were causing severe bloating, and his body was filling up with toxins. A few days into the hospital stay, Andrew was so swollen he gained 15 pounds of pure water weight. His legs looked like massive tree trunks.

Andrew refused any visitors other than his mom and me, so his family and my family sat in a waiting room together for hours. This was the first time my mom and grandma had a chance to meet his aunts and grandfather. Andrew's mom and I would rotate our visits to his room and come out to give the group updates.

It was shocking to see how quickly his body was shutting down. While he was in the ICU, the nurse put a bedpan under him when he needed to go, because he couldn't turn on his side to wipe himself. He could barely move because his stomach was so bloated it looked like it was filled with boulders. One time I had to put gloves on to wipe his butt for him because he refused to let a nurse clean him up. Andrew was humiliated by this. Even though I knew it was serious, I could not stop laughing. I think I was nervously laughing, but Andrew certainly did *not* appreciate my reaction. How mad could he have been, though? I was literally cleaning his ass like he was an infant.

For the first three days in the ICU, Andrew wasn't given anything to eat or drink because his body couldn't process anything. One day he was so frustrated he begged a nurse for something to eat, and she brought him half a cup of ice chips.

At one point he had a procedure to attach a medical bag to his side to collect all the toxins and waste that were filling up his body. When he was moved to a regular room, his roommate was a recent amputee. The doctors were constantly changing the roommate's wraps due to an infection. It smelled like death. I'd walk into the room and it would smell of rot, like there was a decomposing dead animal in there. Sometimes I didn't know if the smell was coming from Andrew or his roommate.

For the pain, the doctors were giving him oxycodone, hydromorphine, and lorazepam. One day I pulled the nurses aside and told them he had a serious drug addiction and these pills were not good for him.

"Right now we are dealing with his pancreatitis, and this is what he needs," was their response.

They looked at me and treated me like I was a dumb junkie girl-friend. I begged them to change his medicine to anything that was not an opiate. I'd call the hospital after I left trying to speak to a new nurse, anyone that would listen to me. Nobody took my 26-year-old self seriously. Andrew would set his alarm for every four hours so he'd be awake to request more drugs. Even confined to a hospital bed, he figured out a way to remain high.

I visited him every night but went home to take care of Cayman and work during the day. I tried to stay focused at work, but of course I couldn't. Andrew would call to give me daily updates from his team of doctors, and I would run out at five o'clock on the dot to be with him.

I was still angry at him for cheating on me and was mad that his addictions had gotten so bad that he was in this position, but as always, my love for him superseded everything else.

One day his mom took me outside the hospital. "Hil, I know you love him, but you don't have to stay with him. You've been through enough, and you should go live your life."

There was never a question of me leaving.

I looked at her and said, "I'm prepared to plan either a funeral or a wedding."

31

A HIDDEN PART OF MY LIFE WAS NOW EXPOSED

After two weeks, the doctors cleared Andrew to come home. Aside from both times in rehab, his hospital stay was the longest stretch of time he'd been off heroin and alcohol in over four years. Even though he was taking the pills the hospital was administering to him, I still thought we were moving in the right direction. The optimist in me thought that maybe this was the start of him staying clean. Before he was discharged, a group of doctors and nurses came in to speak to us.

"Andrew, you have a case of acute pancreatitis. You can never drink alcohol again. If you do, it will turn into severe pancreatitis, and 50 percent of people with severe pancreatitis die."

I listened closely, but all I kept thinking was, *Oh great. Tell an alcoholic/drug addict they can never drink again, what are they going to do? Drugs.*

We got home and Cayman was so happy to see her daddy. We spent a few days relaxing, and then our landlord told us she had to speak to us. She proceeded to say that she was refinancing her house and since our apartment was illegal, we had to move out by the end of the month. *You have to be kidding me!*

I immediately started looking for apartments, because finding one was difficult since we had a pit bull. People were so prejudiced and uneducated about the breed, as soon as I would tell someone we had her, they would immediately hang up on me. Cayman was sweeter, gentler, and more trustworthy than most five-pound Chihuahuas, but no one cared.

A few days later I left for work, but when I got to the driveway, I had a flat tire. *Just my luck!* I texted a picture to my manager and told him I'd be late. I called AAA and waited. While I was waiting for them to arrive, my manager called and told me he had to speak to me. He said he didn't want me to drive all the way to work on a donut to be told what he was about to tell me: I was getting laid off that day.

Within 10 days, Andrew had been released from the hospital, we were told we had to move out of our apartment by the end of the month, and I lost my job. Was my life *ever* going to get better?

The reality was, I was doing absolutely nothing to change my life or make it better. By now my life was completely interwoven with Andrew's. I had lost all sense of individuality. My decisions were based around him; my choices were based around him. My life was falling apart because of *his* addictions, and I still didn't leave him. I had no one to blame but myself. I was at an all-time low.

Andrew had to be off work to recover, so I was worried we'd have no income *and* we were trying to find a new apartment in the midst of all this. My friend Sam knew someone who knew someone who had a pit bull and was moving out of their apartment, so she figured it might work out for us. Within a few days Andrew and I went to see the place. It wasn't anything special, but it would do. Plus, the landlord didn't care about Cayman's breed and we were in a tight time crunch, so we couldn't be picky.

At the same time, I was spending all day every day looking for a new job. I landed myself an interview and, how convenient, the office was less than two miles away from the apartment we had just found! I got the job, and we signed the lease to our new home.

I finally had hope that things were looking up.

———

We weren't moving into the new apartment for a few weeks, and while we were still at our current place, Jen wanted to come over to visit and see how Andrew was doing post-hospital. We were hanging out when Andrew excused himself to take a shower. Some time had passed and I started to get nervous, since all I heard was water running for 20 minutes. I went to the bathroom and checked on him.

Andrew was passed out naked on the toilet, his body leaning against the wall holding him up. His lips were blue. There was a syringe on the floor. His bicep was still wrapped with a homemade tourniquet.

I started to scream, "ANDREW, GET UP!" Jen came running in the room, saw Andrew, and started to scream too.

"JEN! GO GET A BUCKET OF ICE WATER!"

I couldn't believe I was here again. I was yelling and screaming at Andrew, smacking him in the face. My mind kept jumping to the first night this had happened a few years back. He didn't have foam pouring out of his mouth this time, but he was unresponsive. I was in shock that I was dealing with this again.

Part of me wanted to call an ambulance, but another part of me told myself not to. *Just wait one more second, wait one more second.* Clearly not having learned my lesson the first time, I risked his life to keep him out of jail and did not call the paramedics. I still was not in the right state of mind. Cayman was frantically running from one room to the other. She knew something was wrong with her dad.

Jen was panicking and called her cousin who had just completed a rehab program for an opiate addiction.

She was yelling, "WHAT DO WE DO? WHAT DO WE DO? HE ISN'T WAKING UP!"

I kept shaking Andrew and pleading for him to get up. We were frantically pouring buckets of ice water over his head. I was checking his breathing and his eyes. There was a little air coming out of his nose, but not much. His eyes were turning yellow, his lips bluer as each second passed.

Jen's cousin asked if we had Narcan, which I stupidly did not. Then he asked if we had Suboxone. Out loud I said, "Suboxone?" wondering if Andrew had any hidden somewhere in the house.

With his eyes still closed, Andrew mumbled, "Don't give me that." *Phew. He's alive.*

Somehow, in his semi-unconscious mind, Andrew knew that if I did give him Suboxone, it would stop the high he was in the midst of. That was enough to wake him out of his stupor.

Jen was scared. So was I. She sat on the edge of my bed taking deep breaths, trying to calm down. She left a short while after, and we were both emotional. I couldn't believe I had just shared that moment with someone. I felt like a hidden part of my life was now exposed.

After Jen left, Andrew and I sat on opposite ends of the couch in silence. Neither of us knew what to say to each other. Part of me had been expecting him to relapse after the hospital, since I knew he wouldn't be able to cope with the fact that he could never drink alcohol again. The other part of me was at my wits' end. The first time he overdosed I was sad and emotional. This time I was really angry. I knew I was smart, but I knew I was acting stupid. I was frustrated with myself. *Why can't I leave him? Why can't I walk away from this nightmare of a life we're living?* My head and my heart were in direct conflict with one another. My head constantly told me to leave. My heart repeatedly convinced me to stay. The conflict I felt within myself due to this was destructive to my being. I was beginning to resent myself.

There was nothing for Andrew to say to me at this point. "I'm sorry" wasn't cutting it anymore. "I'll never use again" literally meant nothing. I was getting tired of crying all the time, of being sad and lonely. Andrew seemed tired too. This act was getting old. My friends and family would ask me how Andrew was doing after the hospital and I'd say, "He's doing great!" For both of us, lying was more common than telling the truth. But now I felt exposed—Jen knew I was lying to everyone. My secret was out.

Jen was pretty distraught over this. She would have nightmares and constantly reach out to make sure I was okay. She kept telling me that Andrew needed more help and had to go back to rehab.

I would tell her he was fine and she would say, "Hil, are you fucking kidding me? I know he is not fine! I just saw he is not fine!"

A week or two later, Jen said we had to talk. She told me she didn't want to come to my house and I should meet her in a random parking lot, so I knew right off the bat something was wrong. When we met up, Jen told me that even though I was her best friend, she could not support my relationship with Andrew anymore. She said she'd figured out that I must have dealt with him overdosing before based on my initial reaction to get the ice water—which, again, I have no idea why that even worked. She expected me to be in shock and horror, but instead it was like I knew what to do—so she knew I had hidden his first overdose from her. She said I was lying to myself and I was allowing myself to be used and taken advantage of. She told me I used to be the strongest person she knew, and now I was weak.

Jen knew if I was hiding things from *her*, things were bad. And she was right. For months I didn't even tell her that Andrew had cheated on me, since I knew she would be so disappointed. Jen went on to tell me that Andrew was an anchor weighing me down and I deserved to be with someone who would boost me up and bring out all the positive qualities in me. Instead, Andrew was bringing out the worst in me. She told me I had given him so many chances and all he had done to me was lie, cheat, and disappoint; that our relationship was one-sided and I was giving everything but not getting anything in return. She told me that she didn't want to be a part of *his* life anymore, and that she loved me with all her heart but couldn't be a part of my life, with him, anymore.

Jen tried to explain how much it hurt her to say these things, but she felt that she had to.

I waited for her to finish reaming me out and then looked at her with genuine shock and disgust. I felt like she was being the worst friend ever. I couldn't believe she was giving me an ultimatum like this. Jen always had boyfriends, and even if I thought they were shitheads, I would support her. I felt like the one time I was in a relationship, she was telling me she couldn't be there for me.

We angrily both got in our separate cars and drove away from each other. It was the first time in our friendship I felt that she betrayed me. I was wrong. She was being the best friend that I needed.

I shouldn't have expected Jen to support me, because I *was* being different, I *was* lying to myself. And if the tables were turned, I wouldn't have supported her in a relationship like this. But at the time, I could not believe what she was doing.

Jen's brutal honesty had my head spinning for days. She had made her point and she was in my head. Her words would repeat in my mind. *I used to be the strongest person she knew, and now I am weak. She's right. I am weak.*

32

"PLEASE GIVE ME ONE MORE CHANCE"

Shortly after my meetup with Jen, Andrew and I moved into our new apartment. It was hard not speaking to her, but I respected the distance she needed since deep down I knew she was right.

When we moved in, I noticed a large house across the street with multiple families in it. I later found out it was a small Section 8 housing complex. For the record, I have zero issues with anyone living in assisted housing and truly believe that affordable housing programs are underused and need to be more readily available for people who need them. What I had an issue with was the drugs being sold out of this particular house. And then I found out that someone had been murdered in their driveway a few weeks before we moved in. *MURDERED?! You have to be kidding me that this is where we ended up!*

This didn't make any sense to me, considering my new job was less than two miles away in an upscale neighborhood called Huntington Village. Our apartment was in Huntington Station, and although that was a different town, it was close enough to the Village that we thought it was safe. Andrew and I were locked into a lease, so I hoped for the best.

Three weeks after we moved in, Andrew left to catch a train to get to work. I was in front of my mirror putting on makeup when my phone started to ring. It was Andrew. I assumed he'd missed the train.

"What's up?" I answered, annoyed.

Andrew was hysterically crying on the other end of the phone. I could barely understand him. I thought someone in his family had died, the way he was sobbing.

"Andrew, what's wrong? I can't understand you. Are you okay?"

Through his tears, Andrew told me he needed help.

"Hil, it's not even 7:30 in the morning and all I'm thinking about is shooting dope. I am staring at everyone on the train platform, and they are so happy. I don't feel any happiness."

When you love someone with all of your soul, it is crushing to hear that they do not feel any happiness. I told him to come home so we could talk; his tone was making me nervous. I thought he was going to jump in front of a train.

"Honey, if I go get help again, will you please give me one more chance? Will you please stay with me if I go back to rehab? Please give me one more chance," he asked through his cries.

I begged him to come home so we could talk in person. When he got home, he hugged me so tight. He cried like a baby on my shoulder. This was the first and only time I had ever seen him react this way, reflecting on his own addiction. I don't know what set him off this particular morning, but I was internally grateful that something did. I told him to stay home and that I had to think about it. I already knew I would stick by him, but I was trying to play hardball. I went to work and tried to focus, remembering this was my new job and I couldn't mess it up. When I got home that night, I told him this would be the last time I would stand by him.

"I will do this one more time, but if you go to rehab and come back and relapse again, I am leaving you for good."

Andrew was relieved to know I would give him one more chance and stay by his side, again. He may not have deserved it, but I loved him and wanted him to get better—I needed him to get better. Andrew told me that he didn't want to go back to a 12-Step program since they had not worked for him. He researched other options and looked up "non-12-Step programs near the beach." Andrew had always loved the beach and the ocean, and he thought that would be a good environment for his recovery. Seeing him voluntarily looking into getting help on his own gave me hope. I let him run with it. Neither of us knew that our lives were in the process of dramatically changing, finally for the better.

Andrew found a facility that looked incredible located in Pensacola, Florida, housed in a big, beautiful building that was literally *on* the beach—I'll refer to the program as GBR. The website's home page said, "When was the last time you woke up happy? Make the Choice to End Chronic Relapse of Alcohol Abuse and Drug Addiction Today." This was certainly fitting for Andrew.

He was intrigued and called to get more information. A kind man named Reed answered the phone and started asking Andrew about his story. We were told that their program was considered "transformational" instead of "traditional." Reed explained to Andrew that GBRs program was based around an approach known as the Three Principles: Mind, Consciousness and Thought. They did not accept insurance and required a two-month program commitment. The 12-Step programs Andrew had tried in the past had been insurance-based. It always blew my mind that when Andrew was at rehab, once a week his counselor had to call his insurance company to speak to a random stranger who knew nothing about Andrew, and that individual would somehow determine whether Andrew was approved for the following seven days.

GBR was different. Reed told Andrew they did not go through insurance for that exact reason. They felt that the most success came through a solid two-month program, and they didn't want a stranger determining when Andrew was finished; he would be finished when the program was complete. The entire concept sounded amazing, until we asked how much it cost, and nearly passed out. The answer was $25,000.

"HOW ARE WE SUPPOSED TO AFFORD THAT? WE ARE 26 YEARS OLD!" I shrieked.

Andrew spent an hour on the phone with Reed, jotted down more information, and hung up. He really felt that this was the place for him. We called his mom and told her what was happening, that Andrew had relapsed again and this was his plan to move forward.

A few years before this, Andrew's grandmother had passed away and left him a trust account with a large amount of money in it, but he would not have access to it until he turned 30. His mom told us there was a provision in the trust for funds to be pulled out for education or medical emergencies. This was considered an emergency, and he could use the trust to pay for the program if he wanted to.

One side of me believed that everything happened for a reason and this could save his life. The other part of me, the one that had always struggled so much financially, couldn't believe he just "found" this much money.

I understand the complete and utter unfairness of this situation. If Andrew hadn't had this money from his grandmother, he likely would have died. I was shocked that a program so beneficial for addicts was essentially unattainable for the majority of people who needed it. It made me realize that the medical system and rehabilitation programs need a complete overhaul. Programs like this need to be accessible for anyone seriously looking for help. Instead of throwing addicts in jail, we should be spending money on rehabilitating them. Most addicts only commit crimes to feed their addiction, not because they are bad people or criminals at heart.

Andrew called back GBR and started setting up his plans to go. I was happy and sad at the same time. I was used to driving an hour to visit when Andrew was in a 28-day rehab. Now he was going to be 1,500 miles away, and for twice the length of time.

I told myself I was resilient and to stay strong. It sounded good, but was easier to say than do.

33

GBR

Andrew's flight to Florida was booked for a few days later. I drove him to the airport and cried my eyes out while we hugged goodbye.

"Andrew, you have to get better this time, for you first, and then for me. You are making a huge financial investment right now and you need to stay focused."

He assured me that he would and told me he loved me more than anything. We cried in each other's arms. Both of us were emotionally drained and overwhelmed. He thanked me for sticking by him through this. I could not believe he was about to leave for rehab for a third time and would be so far from me. I was inconsolable as I watched him walk away.

I sat in my car and cried alone for what seemed like hours. I wanted to believe that the "third time was the charm," but I was doubtful. I tried to find the courage to make it through the next two months. I loved him so much, I would have done anything for him. I needed him to do this for me. I needed him to do this for us. I didn't know how much longer I could deal with feeling so sad all the time. I was running out of steam. His addiction was exhausting, and I was beyond exhausted.

Little did I know, I had just entered a Forever Haze of After.

———

A few days before Andrew left, I had reached out to Jen and told her that she was right. Andrew did need help and was going back to rehab. When I got back to my apartment from the airport, Jen was waiting outside my house. She was waiting to do what best friends do and support me while I spent the next two months alone. I got out of the car and she came up to me and gave me a hug, telling me it was going to be okay and that she was there for me. Her showing up at my house, after what had transpired the last time we saw each other, was one of the truest moments of pure friendship and love I have ever experienced.

Aside from Jen, Andrew's and my immediate families, and a few close friends, no one knew Andrew was in rehab. I told everyone he was "working" in Florida for two months. I don't know how anyone believed me, since his job was based in New York, but as always, I hid the truth of his addiction.

Andrew was in the detox wing for a few days and couldn't contact me. When he finally did call, he sounded great. He told me that this detox program was different from anything he had previously experienced. When he felt he was ready to move out of detox, he received a medical evaluation and they agreed he could transfer to the next phase. This was a key difference. Andrew was actually part of his program instead of being moved along in a systematic "one size fits all" approach. Another big difference was that at the other rehab, they had given him narcotics or Suboxone to detox. At GBR, they were giving him sauna treatments and non-narcotic muscle relaxers to help with his muscle spasms, which were a symptom of heroin withdrawal.

"A sauna treatment? What is that?" I asked.

He explained that a nurse would take him to a sauna where he'd sit for two to three hours a day and sweat out the toxins in his body. Every 30 minutes he would get out so the nurse could take his blood pressure, weigh him, and check other vitals to make sure he was properly hydrated and that his body was reacting okay. I really liked the idea of this holistic approach.

Andrew continued to call me every day to check in, and he sounded better each time. One day I asked him how he was feeling, and his response was, "I feel incredible." *Incredible? I've never heard him use that word before.* It gave me hope.

GBR encouraged me to take virtual group therapy sessions with the parents and loved ones of other people in their program. The leader of the class explained some of the differences between GBR's approach and a traditional 12-Step approach. What I learned was a real eye-opener.

12-Step programs assume addiction is permanent and can only be controlled. GBR believes that once someone reaches a higher level of understanding through personal insight, addictive behaviors will be removed from their lifestyle. 12-Step tells you that recovering from addiction is hard work and you will need to keep going to meetings for your entire life, but GBR believes that people can and do change and are able to fully recover and live life free of addiction. 12-Step says you must relive past experiences to free yourself from symptoms of addiction, but GBR believes that you are more than your past conditioning.

Let me be very clear, 12-Step programs and attending AA and NA are incredibly successful options for many people dealing with addiction. They save a countless number of lives. I know and have met many people who succeed through these programs, and they would be dead without them. But the reality is, it simply did not work for Andrew. It's important to know that if you are struggling with addiction and your recovery isn't working, there are alternative options available; we were lucky to have found one.

After this revealing discussion, Andrew and I spoke about the differences in treatment he was experiencing. He said to me, "Hil, the other rehab would tell me that the hardest day was the day I was going to leave their program and that no matter how long I am clean, I will always be an addict. That I need to work on my addiction every minute of every day for the rest of my life. They told me it would never get easier. And then they'd tell me to try to stay clean while dealing with all of that."

For someone with his level of heightened anxiety, I can see how terrifying that was. I had never looked at the situation from his perspective, and this was mind-blowing to me. You are already an addict, clearly having an issue dealing with whatever situation you're in, and now you're told that this will be you for the rest of your life and it will never get easier? I know and respect a lot of people who need that challenge every day to stay sober, and I admire them for their perseverance. But that angle did not work for Andrew, and I don't know if I would succeed under those conditions either.

Andrew found a mentor in Reed, the same man who answered the phone when Andrew called to inquire about the program. Reed took Andrew under his wing. To this day I credit Reed for being one of the reasons why Andrew is not only alive but thriving. I will always feel indebted to this man, even though I have never met him.

Throughout Andrew's treatment at GBR, he was put on a healthy diet, exercised, and read. He started meditating every morning. He was comforted and supported while diving deep inside himself to learn who he really was, at his roots, at his essence—which, he realized, was *not* an addict. Most importantly, they taught him how to manage his reactions to his thoughts. As an addict, you will get urges to use. That is an inevitable tragedy of addiction. GBR taught him how to accept his thoughts, acknowledge them, and then move on, without giving in to the impulses that follow. This sounds *much* easier than it is to properly integrate with your thinking, but once you do—you could be free.

GBR would say, "If you get an impulse to use drugs or drink, try going outside in the cold weather or taking a cold shower. When your body gets cold, your brain stops thinking about using drugs. Your brain has moved on to its next thought."

This was a breakthrough lesson for Andrew. Previously, once the thought of using entered his mind, he couldn't move past it. He would lie, steal, and cheat his way through to satisfy that craving. Now he was learning to simply accept what he was thinking, not to run from it. Just let it in, let it pass, and move on. This was an incredible lesson for me as well, to learn that your mind is the most powerful "muscle" in your body.

About halfway through the program Andrew was allowed to have a visitor. His mom said she wanted me to go and paid for my flight and hotel, for which I was incredibly grateful. I was so nervous heading to Florida, trying not to feel too hopeful, but excited to see my man for the first time in over a month.

When I arrived at GBR, Andrew walked out to meet me and I instantly saw a change in him. He was in great shape; his eyes were big and wide. His beautiful crystal-blue eyes pierced my heart. He was attentive and he was smiling. He hugged me tight and he felt so strong, I didn't want him to let me go.

The facility allowed Andrew to leave for eight hours with me. This restored a sense of normalcy in Andrew and reassured him that GBR truly believed what they had been telling him all along, that he was not an addict and could be successful out in the real world. Honestly, I was nervous to be responsible for him since it would be his first time out of the rehab and back where triggers, drugs, and alcohol surrounded us. Nevertheless, the facility allowed it, so we made a plan for the day and left.

We got back to my hotel room and made love. He was so present and alert, it felt amazing to be back in his arms. We hadn't been intimate while sober in years. This felt different. This felt real. Afterward I took a shower before we headed out for the day. When I got out of the shower, he was not in the hotel room. I started to panic. *Oh my God, he's down at the hotel bar getting drunk. He found a drug dealer and is already high. How could I leave him alone like that?*

I threw on my clothes and was about to run downstairs to try and find him. Suddenly through the curtains, I saw his foot on the balcony. I ran over and there he was, sitting on a chair, smoking a cigarette, reading a book called *Become What You Are.*

What the hell? He's reading? Aside from a high school textbook, I had never seen him read—and a philosophy book, no less? That was another sign that he was changed.

"Hey, babe! Ready for our day?" he said cheerfully.

I was *so* ready. I looked down six stories off our balcony, and in the sand I saw "I LOVE HIL." It was adorable. Here I was thinking he was off somewhere shooting up; meanwhile he'd snuck out to write me a cheesy cute note in the sand like we were seven years old.

We spent the day laughing at the beach, going out to lunch, laughing and kissing along the way. We had a nice dinner on the water and talked about his program and our relationship. It was one of the first times we were communicating soberly, openly, and truthfully. Andrew seemed very different. He finally seemed like the man I had been waiting for. Although part of me tried to remain reserved and hesitant, the other part of me was more than ready to embrace this version of him.

After dinner I dropped him off at GBR, and he told me I could come back the following day to meet his counselor and have a tour of the place. I got back to the hotel and stretched out on the bed, staring at the ceiling, in awe of the transformation I had seen.

The next day I got to the facility early, excited to spend my last day with Andrew. We met with his counselor to talk about life post-rehab. She explained that if I wanted to stay with Andrew, my life would need to change as well. She said that I had to be able to move on from his addiction and forgive him in totality, instead of trying to get individual resolutions for all the wrongs he'd done in the past.

Although I was ecstatic to see he was changing, I was resistant to this. I thought Andrew was getting off easy by not having to apologize to me for each individual time he had hurt me so deeply. I wanted to know the truth behind each lie and the reason behind each relapse. I thought I needed a thorough explanation of why he had cheated on me. But it was foolish to think that would get us to where we needed to be. And my approach would have taken a *long* time.

By the end of the session, Andrew gave me one comprehensive, thorough, meaningful apology that I knew came from the heart. He was emotional and direct. I knew he meant it, and I knew he was sorry for all he had done to me. Part of me was still hurt from the years of lies and mistrust, but I had to do what his counselor said in order to make our relationship successful once he left rehab.

Of course, Andrew's actions in the past mattered, but the reasons behind his actions mattered too. Andrew didn't do the things he did because he wanted to hurt me or because he didn't love me. He did what he did because he was an addict. Because he would literally do anything to feed his destructive itch to use. I had to be understanding and compassionate toward that. For years, he was not in control. His addiction was. I knew I wanted to be with him for the rest of my life, so I had to accept his apology for everything he'd done and really feel in my heart that I could move on with him and not look back.

That is exactly what we did.

34

COMING HOME

I got back to New York, excited and ready to start our life post-rehab. I still had one problem looming, though. The neighborhood we lived in was getting worse. One Friday night, Cayman was at the back window whining and barking, which she never did. I looked outside and there were flashlights shining everywhere. I heard police radios in my yard, so I called the police station, and they told me there was a drug raid around the corner and people were running from the cops. In the town, no one had fences in their backyards, so it was an open area. The police told me to stay inside until the next morning.

Great, first a murder across the street, drug deals happening every hour in their driveway, and now a drug raid around the corner. I knew that Andrew could not come home to this house. We'd be setting him up for failure.

By now I was working for real estate attorneys and told them my predicament. As soon as I told them where I lived, they said, "Why in the world would you move to *that* street?" I had no idea it was a known bad area, but apparently it was. I told them I didn't feel safe living there but we were locked into a lease. They helped me come up with a legal basis to get out of the lease without penalty. Meanwhile, Andrew's mom was renting an apartment she never used and got approval for us to take over the lease with Cayman. Her apartment was within walking distance of the beach, which would be a perfect place for Andrew to live, considering his rehab was on the beach and it was a calming environment for him.

I spent the next month preparing for Andrew to come home and reading some of the self-help books that GBR recommended. It was nice not to feel tense and angry all the time. The feeling of hope, after years of feeling hopeless, was empowering. For once, I felt in sync with myself. Finally, my head and my heart were in agreement.

The day Andrew came home, we were both as nervous as we were excited. When I picked him up at the airport, he looked like a different man than the one I had dropped off two months earlier. I broke down when I saw him. I was over the moon he was home, but of course I was nervous that he was now out of the comforting confines of rehab. When we got to our apartment, Cayman was running in circles, so excited her dad was home.

Within the first few days of being back, Andrew asked me to take him to the phone store to change his number so people from his past wouldn't be able to contact him. He also went through his closet and threw out the majority of his wardrobe and fitted baseball hats. He wanted to move away from the image of his old self. These were both clear differences from the prior times when Andrew had gotten home from rehab. He was taking steps in the right direction.

From the day that he got home, he was waking up early to meditate before he started his day. He never watched TV and was constantly reading books to further his understanding of himself. He was borrowing my car for the first few weeks, since he had sold his after his second arrest. Although I was nervous about him relapsing, I knew I had to trust him in order for this to work. He was doing all the right things, and I had to let everything play out. Andrew was not only clean and sober; he was clean, sober, and happy. When the time came, we packed up the apartment and moved to our new place. My commute changed from a 3-mile to an 80-mile round-trip. Andrew's sobriety was worth it.

Around the same time as our move to the beach, Andrew got

himself a car and a job. Things were starting to happen, and they were finally good things.

35

"AM I A HORRIBLE WOMAN?"

One Friday night in October, I got home from work and Andrew said we had to talk. I panicked, thinking he had relapsed. He assured me he hadn't, but there was something on his mind. He explained that he'd realized he did not want kids and didn't want this to become an issue between us in the future. Basically, he said he wasn't sure if we should stay together since we felt differently about something so important.

I felt like the rug had been pulled from underneath me.

Although I guess I had always pictured myself as a mom, I certainly was *not* thinking about it during this time in our lives. I was blindsided by him bringing this up, especially because things had been so good between us since he had gotten home. At this point we had been together for four years and he had struggled with addiction almost the entire time. He had been home and sober for less than three months.

Andrew tried to explain to me that our lives were moving toward marriage, but he wanted to make sure I knew where he stood on this before we made that commitment. I felt like he was giving up on me after I had waited for him and stood by him for years. I couldn't believe he was suddenly focusing on an issue that could break us apart

—or was he looking for a way out? Whichever it was, I couldn't stay in the apartment with him at that moment.

I called Jen, and Andrew and I spent the night apart. The next morning I started crying before my eyes even opened. I couldn't imagine not being with Andrew, not waking up to him every day. I felt that after how strong I had been for him, how much bad shit I'd stuck through, I deserved the best version of him. And for that reason, and because I loved him, I wasn't ready to let go—especially because having children was so far from my mind at that time. For the first time, I was getting to experience a small taste of the relationship I had always envisioned. And I wanted more of it.

Andrew picked me up from Jen's so we could talk, since he was just as unhappy as I was about how our night had unfolded.

"You just got back from rehab and told me you take one day at a time and live in the present, so how can you tell me now that you know with certainty what you will want in the future?" I asked.

This statement may appear manipulative, but I didn't mean it that way. It was the truth. I didn't understand how "one day at a time" and "I never want children" could both be in his mind at the same time. Andrew agreed he was not ready to give up on our relationship either. We decided to stay together and revisit this down the road.

———

After our kid talk, our relationship got back on track. We spent our days laughing and hanging at the beach, which was only a three-minute walk away. We started to garden and to ride bikes. I stopped drinking for a few years to support Andrew and his recovery. Everything we did, we did sober. Talking, laughing, disagreeing, our sex life —it all changed, and it changed for the better.

After a few months of this bliss, I realized that I had missed my period. Since I was on birth control, I didn't think too much of it and let it go. The next month came, no period. I started to panic.

Andrew went to the store and bought me a pregnancy test. The second I peed on the stick, a plus sign came up. I sat on the toilet in silence and in shock. *Holy shit. I cannot believe this.*

I was in there for too long. Andrew opened the bathroom door nervously. He looked at the stick and we stared at each other in silence. I had always pictured that when I found out I was pregnant it would be a joyous and exciting moment. This situation could not have felt more opposite to that.

Andrew looked at me and broke the ice. "Listen, we can do whatever you want us to do."

"Whatever *I* want us to do?" I said, annoyed. "Andrew, months ago you told me you basically wanted to break up since you didn't want children. Now you're telling me we can do whatever *I* want?"

Andrew told me he wanted to be supportive and didn't want to make any decisions for me; that it was my body and my choice, and he'd be there no matter what I chose to do. I went outside and called Jen, trying to get my thoughts together.

"Jen, I am freaking out. I just took a pregnancy test, and it's positive!"

Since I had gone to Jen's the night of my talk with Andrew about having kids, she knew this was a sensitive subject. She told me to take a deep breath and said no matter what decision I made, she would help us through it. Then she told Andrew to go get me ice cream.

I went back inside and sat on the couch, still silent and in my own head. I could not believe that I was pregnant. I had $150 in my checking account, no savings account, was just starting life with sober Andrew, and we had just spoken about how both of us were not ready for kids. Part of me was confused as to why I was not even considering going through with the pregnancy. *Am I a horrible woman? There isn't one ounce of me that is ready for this right now.*

The reality was, even though Andrew's transformation was obvious, he was only six months out of rehab and I still wasn't totally sure this would last forever. Of course I wanted it to, but I couldn't forget that he'd relapsed so many times before. He had not remained sober for longer than a few months in more than four years. There was so much uncertainty for me at that time, and before bringing a baby into the picture, I needed to be certain. I needed to be certain that my life would no longer consist of finding syringes scattered around the house. I needed to be certain I wouldn't find Andrew unresponsive with a tourniquet around his arm. I needed to be certain that I was ready.

I wasn't certain.

Andrew staying sober and us building a healthy relationship were my focus at the time, not having a baby. By that night, I was sure with every piece of my soul that I could not move forward with the pregnancy. Andrew was relieved but also very supportive and was ready for me to make the decision on my own. I made up my mind.

If it weren't for Jen, I don't know how we would have gotten through this. Andrew and I were both overwhelmed and didn't know how to handle the situation. I wasn't thrilled with my current ob-gyn and was in the process of changing doctors but didn't want this to be the start of a new medical relationship. So, Jen called multiple doctors and clinics for me. She would call us back with a summary of their options and tell us her opinion. She found a place that we were comfortable with, and *she* scheduled my abortion appointment. As with most times in my life, she was my rock. Other than the staff at the clinic, Jen, Andrew, and I were the only people who knew I was pregnant.

The morning of the abortion, Jen met us at our apartment and the three of us drove to my appointment. The doctor said I needed to have a sonogram, and I felt like I was going to be sick. I didn't want to know any details. I wanted them to cover my eyes and ears and just get it over with. Andrew was holding my hand, telling me we were going to be okay.

I was going to have an aspiration procedure, which is when they use a vacuum/suction to remove uterine contents. The doctor called me into the room, and I had to go alone. I was nervous but ready. I kept thinking I was such a shitty person, since I never really considered keeping the baby.

I knew I was not ready to have a child, and for that reason, I hid it from my mom. I thought she would be disappointed and sad, and I couldn't let that affect my decision. I made *my* decision, and I couldn't let anyone else's feelings affect me. It wasn't until I wrote this book six years later that she found out about this. When I told her, she completely understood my decision and cried because I'd gone through it without her support. I should have trusted that she would have been there for me. I could have used my mom during this time.

When I walked into the room, it hit me that it was about to happen. The doctors gave me medicine to help me relax and told me the procedure would take a few minutes and feel like severe cramping. When it started, I couldn't believe the pain. I kept trying to distract my mind, to not think about the fact that a fetus was being suctioned out of my body. A tear rolled down my face as I stared at the wall. I felt guilty but also weirdly relieved. I knew in my heart this was the right decision, for me.

The process was over in less than two minutes. I had the severe cramping pains they warned me of but couldn't believe how little time it took to terminate a pregnancy. Something so big, so life changing, was done in 120 seconds.

When I got back to the waiting room, Andrew was pacing back and forth. He and Jen both hugged me and we left, not saying much. I sat in the backseat on the ride home, and Jen and Andrew were constantly turning around to make sure I was okay. At one point, while we were on a parkway, I yelled, "Pull over, quickly!" I started throwing up out the window. I don't know if it was from the procedure or from nerves, but I needed a minute to get myself together on the side of the road.

We got home and Jen and Andrew gave me ice cream and junk food, and we watched movies. I tried to keep my mind busy, but I kept thinking, *I can't believe I just had an abortion and didn't tell my mom.*

Two days later, I was back at work, and life went on.

36

"IT'S NOT MY MESSAGE"

While working for the real estate attorneys, I became close with my coworker Cindy. She was very spiritual and had an ability to feel energies and hear things that other people couldn't. She didn't consider herself a psychic, but she was able to connect with the energies of people who had passed and she felt intuitions about things, which were usually spot on.

A few months before the day I'm about to describe, Cindy and I were at lunch and she randomly asked me, "Hil, are you pregnant?" I had not told anyone other than Andrew and Jen, and my abortion appointment was the following week. I looked at her blankly and didn't respond, obviously caught off guard. She said, "It's okay, I just felt it. Let me know if you need anything." From that moment on, I trusted that her feelings and intuitions were legitimate.

Cindy knew my story about Jon, and I told her often about the rainbows Jen and I had seen and the messages we felt. By this time, Jon had been gone more than seven years, but my stories still flowed out of me. Cindy and I connected through this since I felt comfortable speaking to her about it, knowing she wouldn't think I was crazy.

One Friday afternoon at work, Cindy went up to the copy machine and hit the start button. The lights and computers all flickered and I saw Cindy duck out of the way, almost as if she'd seen something from the corner of her eye about to fly into her. The lights flickered again.

Cindy, our two other coworkers, and I looked at each other, confused about what had just happened. We felt a weird energy in the room and we all had goosebumps on our arms. Something was in there with us.

Cindy said out loud, "It's me, John, and I am okay. It's me and I am okay."

We stared back at Cindy. "Cin, who is John? What is going on?" I asked.

"Did you guys hear that?" she asked, while looking around the room.

None of us knew what she was talking about. Cindy then told us that right before the lights flickered, she'd felt a surge of energy behind her and had heard someone say, "It's me, John, and I am okay."

Cindy looked at me. "Hil, could this be Jonny telling me he is okay?"

"Ummm, I don't think so. No. He already told me he is okay."

I was sure of it. I had received my messages years earlier. I saw a rainbow moments after I asked for a sign. I was told by a girl I barely knew that Jon had visited her in her sleep and instructed her to tell "Hil's crew" that he was chillin' and had his wings. Then a stranger told me that in life I might not always have money but I would always have my rainbows. I already knew Jon was okay. This John was not my Jon. This was not my message.

The energy in the room among all of us was electrifying. We were a little spooked, but it's hard to explain the feeling. I went outside for a smoke break in an attempt to recalibrate my brain so I could finish the day. For some reason I walked directly across the street from my office, which was not where I usually stood and smoked. I normally tried to stay out of sight from my building, but that day, I walked right across the street.

Cindy and I always got in trouble for taking smoke breaks together, but within seconds she followed me outside. My lack of reaction to that experience had caused her to think I was upset. Just like when I saw my rainbow with Jen at college right after I asked for my sign—no reaction. Sometimes I need to deal with things internally before being able to express them externally.

"Hil, I'm really sorry if I upset you. I'm not sure what happened in there, but someone named John just sent me a message to relay to someone."

"Cin, I'm not upset at all. I wish we knew who that message was for. I just needed a minute to get my thoughts together."

We started talking about what had just happened, how Cindy had felt the energy so strongly she'd had to duck out of its way. I started talking about my story again; whenever I got into the rainbows, it was like I got a surge of adrenaline. Something ignited in me. It was a spiritual moment, and we felt connected. Very unusually, I lit a second cigarette as soon as I finished my first. I never did that.

As I took the first drag, from around the corner a well-dressed, nice-looking woman approached us smiling.

"Hi, ladies, is this the smoking section?"

She asked for a lighter and started to chit-chat with us. We were making small talk, and I asked her if she worked in the neighborhood.

"No, I'm from Florida, but I'm up here having lunch with my daughters."

"Well, you picked a beautiful time to visit! Are you having a good time?" Cindy asked.

The woman proceeded to tell us that she was celebrating her husband, who had recently passed away. Her children lived in New York, so she had come to have a celebration-of-life party with them.

Goosebumps filled my body. In my head I kept telling myself, *You have to ask her what his name was! Maybe this message is for her. You have to ask!* I looked at Cindy; she looked back at me. We both looked at this woman, whom neither of us had ever seen before until this moment.

"Was your husband's name John, by any chance?" I blurted out. I had to know.

She looked at me surprised but didn't say anything for a few moments. "What are you, a psychic or something?"

I started to laugh and patted Cindy on her back. "No, but my friend is!"

By the look on her face, I could tell the woman was getting emotional. We all looked at each other in awkward silence. Cindy would later tell me that at this exact moment, she felt another surge of energy and envisioned a large table with 10 people sitting around it.

Cindy took a deep breath and looked directly at the woman.

"I received a message that John is okay. He said he is here, and he is okay. I saw a big table with 10 people around it, I don't know why. But he is okay. He's told me three times."

The woman stared at Cindy in awe and shock. She looked at me. I was smiling, but quiet. I knew the message was not my message. The woman asked if she could give us a hug. Here we were, total strangers, hugging on a street corner.

After our hug, she told us that her husband was a former New York City firefighter who was a very strong man and had been fighting cancer for years. He was truly afraid to die and fought in agony for several months. Toward the end of his life, all *10* of their children traveled to Florida to see him before he passed. She told us that at the very end, he had suffered so much, but kept fighting because he was too afraid to die. She eventually found the courage to say to him, "You're going to be okay. I promise you're going to be okay." He passed away shortly after that.

The woman looked at us as tears filled her eyes. "You know, leave it to my John to make me come all the way to freaking New York for a cigarette just for him to let me know he is finally okay."

We all laughed, and she asked if she could give us another hug. As she was walking away, she said, "My daughters are waiting for me at the restaurant. They are *never* going to believe what just happened to me. Thank you so much."

Cindy and I watched this woman walk away and turn the corner, never to be seen again. I like to think that because I was in *my* Forever Haze of After, I was able to help her get to *her* After, now knowing her husband was okay and at rest. I'm confident this woman has never forgotten this moment, just like I haven't. It was beautiful and mystical.

I do not know what happens after someone dies. What I will tell you is that the events of this day happened in a celestial way. There is no chance that any one moment of that day was a coincidence. If I had never had my spiritual experience, if I had never opened myself up to the possibility that I was receiving messages, I never would have been able to help pass this message on. If Cindy hadn't told us what she heard, we would not have been outside when we were. If I hadn't gone outside to smoke a cigarette, if I hadn't stood in a place I never had before, if I hadn't lit the second cigarette, we never would have met this woman. And if we had never met this woman, we never would have known whose message it was.

It was not my message. It was hers.

37

"WILL YOU MARRY ME?"

Full disclosure: Andrew smokes weed. I don't want people thinking I haven't been truthful by claiming he's remained sober, which I wholeheartedly stand behind. I understand some people consider weed a drug and a mind-altering substance. I personally do not, nor do I look at his smoking as the lesser of two evils. Andrew did not start shooting heroin because he smoked weed. Andrew uses weed and meditation to help deepen his life experiences. It allows him to work through his anxieties and restless mind, without resorting to traditional psychotherapy or antidepressants. He leads a well-balanced, all-natural lifestyle. Since he attended GBR, he has never shot heroin, taken any pills (not even painkillers after having all his wisdom teeth removed), or had one sip of alcohol. Tobacco, opiates, and alcohol kill millions of people every single year. In the history of the world, weed has killed zero people. To me and his loved ones, Andrew is sober; and smoking a plant does not make me any less proud of him.

———

The next two years were some of the best of times for Andrew and me. By the summer of 2016, we had been together for six years, and the last two of them he remained sober. We loved our life together, and everything that was happening was positive. Andrew cut off 95 percent of the people he'd previously hung out with. We didn't have many friends, since it was hard to find other 28-year-olds who weren't drinking and spending their weekends at the bars. We both quit smoking cigarettes and I stopped taking Adderall, which I had continued to take since leaving college. We traveled to the Cayman Islands, Costa Rica, Punta Cana—we were healthy, thriving, and happy.

Andrew and I didn't talk about marriage much but both knew we'd be together forever. I was okay with our relationship because I knew Andrew's journey was a long one, and I didn't want to pressure him into thinking I needed more. He was fully committed to me and his sobriety, and I didn't need a ring to prove that.

Since the day Andrew had gotten out of rehab, he had woken up every morning at 6 a.m. and would start his day by meditating and drinking Japanese tea. Unlike graduates of other programs, Andrew was not attending AA or NA meetings or surrounding himself with other addicts in recovery. His morning routine kept him clearheaded, focused, and in touch with himself. He read books any spare moment he had, whether it was on philosophy, self-help, gardening, cooking, how to make cheese or jam, etc. He was *always* reading, *always* working on bettering himself. If he wanted to learn how to do something, he did it 150 percent. He is still that way today.

I spent time reflecting on the events of the last six years. It was fascinating for me to watch Andrew's transformation. Although his addiction seemed far behind us, I couldn't truly comprehend how he was so totally different. One day I said to him, "Babe, I know we don't speak about it much, but do you ever think about using? Do you ever think about how you were a severe addict just a few years ago?"

Andrew sighed and shrugged his shoulders. "Honestly, not really. When I was a kid, I used to play baseball. I don't think about that time in my life anymore. Just like when I was using and drinking. That was my past. I don't think about that time in my life anymore either."

I was dumbstruck by his response. I couldn't fathom that he was comparing years of heroin abuse and alcoholism to playing baseball as a kid. I knew what he meant—that these past chapters in his life were in the past—but I was so used to hearing people in recovery having to relive those moments to stay sober. I couldn't believe the stark difference in Andrew.

I walked over and gave him a hug. "Baby, I am so proud of you and how far you have come."

———

On July 3, 2016, I woke up early to go to the bathroom but couldn't wait to get back into bed. It was the Sunday of the holiday weekend. We had plans later in the day, but my first plan was to sleep in.

I was walking back to the bedroom when Andrew yelled to me from the living room, "Hil, come in here and look at the new collar I bought Cayman!"

"Babe, it's 8 a.m.! I'm going back to bed. I'll look later."

"No, come in now!"

I was annoyed and wanted to get back to sleep. Andrew was always so cheery in the morning, but I needed more time to acclimate to the day. I walked into the living room and Cayman was lying in the middle of the floor with a new purple collar on.

"Go look at it!"

I walked over and leaned down, rubbing my eyes, still half asleep, confused as to why he had even bought her a new collar and why I had to look at it at that exact moment.

"What does her collar say?" I asked.

Then I read the letters: "M A R R Y M E ?"

"Andrew, oh my God, WHAT?"

I turned around and Andrew was on one knee. "Honey, I love you. Will you marry me?"

I hadn't even brushed my teeth yet. It was eight o'clock in the morning, and I was in shock.

"I've been so anxious all morning about this! I couldn't wait any longer," Andrew told me.

To me, this was the most romantic proposal he could have made. I wish he had waited until I'd brushed my teeth, but aside from that, it was perfectly us. It was just us with Cayman, who had to be a part of it since she's like our child. Andrew had the entire day planned. My mom and grandma came over for a celebratory toast. He told me that he and Jen had been ring shopping for a few weeks, so Jen was in on the surprise as well. It was a moment I will never forget.

Ever since I was 12 years old, I knew I would marry Andrew. Like I told his mom outside the hospital, I was prepared to plan a funeral or a wedding.

I got the wedding.

38

MY FOREVER HAZE OF: HE IS RECOVERED

Gearing up to plan the wedding was an emotional process for me, although I didn't show it. I spent time by myself, trying to grasp how different Andrew and I were from just a few years back. I couldn't believe what we had accomplished. I couldn't believe we'd made it. I couldn't believe that he'd survived, that I'd survived.

One day while Andrew was at work, I walked to the beach and gazed at the ocean. I watched the waves crash and remembered a time I was at a Nar-Anon meeting while Andrew was in rehab. A man told me I couldn't control Andrew's addiction just like I couldn't control the waves. It was hard for me to remember those times, to remember how bad a place we were in.

I sat on the sand, digging my toes in. I let my feelings come as they wanted. I let it all out. I cried by myself, tears of joy, of achievement, of sadness, of relief. Andrew and I went from battling each other every single day to having one of the tightest, healthiest relationships I'd ever seen in two people. He is my best friend. We have such a sense of companionship and togetherness. We climbed out of deep holes and over large mountains to get to where we were. I knew in my heart that after some of the shit we had overcome, we could get through anything together.

I realized then that the moment I dropped Andrew off at the airport to go to rehab, the moment I sat in my car crying alone, trying to find the strength to stick by him; that moment, I was in a Forever Haze of After—and I didn't even know it. Since that moment, Andrew has never had a drink or drug. From that moment I would never have to deal with the heartache and pain of loving an addict, because he would no longer be one when I next saw him. For so many years, Andrew's addiction kept us under a dark, dark cloud, but now we were under a clear sky full of sunshine.

Andrew's addiction changed my life because I am now more empathetic toward other addicts I hear about or know. He is a perfect example of why you shouldn't just write off an addict as "unfixable" or "broken." The truth is, it didn't matter that I loved Andrew unconditionally every minute of every day. He only got better when he, himself, decided he wanted to get better. The only difference between Andrew and someone who dies due to an addiction is that Andrew survived until the day he decided to change. When I hear of someone overdosing and passing away, I get sad for them. I'm sad that they didn't have the opportunity to make it to the day *they* would have decided to change. Andrew lives a beautiful life, and people who first meet him are truly shocked to hear about his past. If he had bought one bad bag, filled up one bad needle—all he'd be is a statistic. Now, he's a rare statistic. Now, he's a survivor.

I understood that day at the beach that Andrew's story is unique, that most people who shoot heroin 10 times a day for years don't make it out alive. I believed that he was on a path and was so strong in his own skin, in his own mind, that I would not have to worry ever again about him destroying his life or relapsing. I was in a Forever Haze of After—a good one, a really good one.

I realized in that moment that I was not about to marry a man who was in recovery.

I was about to marry a man who was recovered.

39

LET THE PLANNING BEGIN

In early 2017, we started looking into wedding venues. We both wanted a casual, outdoorsy vibe. After checking out a few locations, we found a place out east on Long Island that was on a lake. It would be a perfect venue for our outdoor wedding. We booked the Sunday afternoon of Labor Day weekend later that year.

Part of me was unsure how to handle our bridesmaids and grooms-men. The reality was, Andrew only had one or two close friends since he had cut off so many people from his past. I had my group of my best girlfriends, but I didn't want him to feel like he had to find random people to fill these made-up positions. That was certainly *not* what this wedding was about to me.

Still, I wanted Jen and my other best friends to be a part of the day in some respect, so I figured out a plan. I told Andrew that we would have a wedding without bridesmaids and groomsmen. I would have my friends act as "honorary" bridesmaids: they didn't have to stand up with us at the altar, they could wear whatever they wanted, but their dresses would somehow coordinate and we would take pictures as a group. I would call them my bridesmaids and they could still take me away for a bachelorette party like they had planned. Basically, they only had to do the fun parts.

I wanted to have Jen as my maid of honor because she had been my rock since the day we sat at Jon's memorial site together. She stood next to me through every up and every down, and I wanted her to be next to me on my wedding day. Andrew had previously told me that when he was seven, he was the best man at his aunt and uncle's wedding. Then I had an idea.

"Babe, why don't you ask your grandpa to be your best man? If you do, I will ask my grandma to be my matron of honor, and then they can be a big part of the wedding."

Andrew was stoked about this idea. His grandpa, whom we all call Pa, was 90 and had been a huge part of raising Andrew after his dad passed away. Since my grandma and I are extremely close, it was perfect to have them fill these important roles. Both of our grandparents gleefully accepted our offers, and just like that, we had our wedding party.

———

During this celebratory time in my life, there was something dreadful looming in the back of my head. I had no idea how I was going to deal with my dad with respect to the wedding. This was something I always knew I would have to deal with, but never knew how I would handle.

I spoke to Brock, and he agreed that it would not be right to have our dad there. It would be awkward for everyone, especially since at that point I hadn't seen him in more than six years. I knew that my mom, as well as my grandma and every other member of my family, would be incredibly uncomfortable if he was there. Andrew had only met him once (aside from when we were kids), and more importantly, *I* would be uncomfortable. And this one day was about me.

I decided to call my dad to tell him I was engaged and that we were planning the wedding. I had a pit in my stomach and thought I was going to throw up. He told me he was happy for me and started asking me details about the wedding date.

I took a deep breath and found the courage to tell him that he wasn't invited. I explained that I didn't think it would be appropriate for him to be there and that I hoped he understood. I even suggested we should pick a weekend to celebrate another time.

Initially, he didn't react as angrily as I had expected. He told me he was disappointed and that he wanted to be there, but it was my decision. Then, he snapped.

"Who the hell is walking you down the aisle? Don't even tell me it's Steven. He is not your father!" he snarled.

In my head I was thinking, *You're not my father either!* But instead, I chose not to argue. I explained that I wasn't sure what I was doing yet. At that moment, my dad didn't even care that he wasn't invited; he cared more about my mom's partner not walking me down the aisle.

The conversation ended civilly and I was relieved it was over. This was a moment I had been dreading, but I did it. Now I could move on.

I was faced with an unanswered question, though: who *was* going to walk me down the aisle? In the Jewish religion, typically both your mom and dad walk you down, so I knew I'd at least have my mom with me.

After one minute of thinking, I figured it out. I picked up the phone.

"Hey, Hil, what's up?" Brock said.

"Brock, you and I have always been so close. We went through so much shit as kids together. I can't think of any other man in my life who'd be suitable for the job. Would you want to walk me down the aisle at my wedding?"

"Hil, I'd be honored. I love you."

That was that. My baby brother was the man walking me down the aisle.

40

"THERE IS A REASON HE IS NOT HERE"

Over the next few months, our wedding plans were set and we were looking forward to the big day. I went dress shopping with my mom and grandma, and although I had a great time, I was super uncomfortable. I absolutely hated being the center of attention and having people look at me. Andrew and I weren't even planning on having a first dance. The thought of all eyes on us made us both want to run and hide.

We were not planning on having a religious wedding, but Andrew agreed that we could be married by a rabbi, sign a ketubah, and have some of the other Jewish traditions as a part of our ceremony. A ketubah is a Jewish marriage contract, which can be decorative and beautiful. When we went to pick one out, we had to fill out paperwork with our parents' information so they could be included in the text. I was uncomfortable listing my dad, since he wasn't a part of my life and wasn't even invited to the wedding. The man who ran the Judaic shop told me it would be "very unusual" to list only my mom. I politely told him my situation was very unusual and I had to think about it.

Part of me felt guilty that I didn't want my dad on there. But I also felt like he didn't help me, at all, in getting to that point in my life.

This was the exact same way I felt about him being at my college grad-uation—he didn't deserve to be a part of these things. I didn't feel it was fair to my mom to have her name listed so close to his, as if they were a union who had raised me together. He didn't really help me accomplish anything, and I didn't know if I wanted his name to be listed on one of the most important documents for the rest of my life.

My mom raised me by herself, and although no one would ever really see or read my ketubah, I felt that she deserved to be listed solely. If anyone else deserved to be with her on there, it was sperm donor C380, because at least he was the other reason I was alive.

Besides deciding to keep my dad off the ketubah, every other aspect of planning the wedding was incredibly easy. No disrespect to any bridezillas out there, but I just didn't understand how people get so wound up over the smallest details. The entire time we planned our wedding, I just kept thinking of how far Andrew and I had come. What color the napkins would be or what the flowers would look like didn't matter to me. Every single vendor I met with told me I was the "chillest" bride they had ever worked with. I never got upset, and Andrew and I never fought.

My girls would text me, "Hil, are you *sure* you are okay? You seem totally fine!"

I was totally fine.

———

The weekend of my wedding, my honorary bridesmaids rented a mansion that was only a few miles from the venue. We partied, barbe-qued, swam, and laughed. I was playing intense beer pong the day before I said "I do." I had some of the best times of my life that week-end. I highly advise anyone getting married to do this. I was occupied the entire weekend leading up to the big day and didn't have a minute to stress out or get worried. I was surrounded by my best friends in a big house with no time to get into my own head.

My dad and I had spoken about my wedding *numerous* times since the day I told him he wasn't invited. Even though I hadn't seen him in years, we agreed that we'd find a date to celebrate together. He assured me he was okay with my decision and wasn't upset. I actually appreciated how understanding he was being. My mistake.

Two days before my wedding, I received a text: *"Hi. Wishing you and Andrew the best of luck. I spoke to your grandmother, she is extremely upset that she and everybody from my side was not invited. You made a poor decision. I thought you were smarter. Love you but I am your father and you have hurt me beyond belief. I will always remember this."*

Rage came over me as I read these manipulative words. I read this text while surrounded by Jen and my other best friends, who loved me and had been there for me through everything the last few years. My dad had been to New York more than 15 times since he'd moved to Florida and never once told me when he was in the same state as I was. He never called to see me. But now, on my wedding weekend, he wanted to tell me *I* had made a poor decision.

To be clear, I had not seen or spoken to his side of the family since I was 17, so it had been over 10 years. They never contacted me, and I never contacted them. One of the last times I saw them, my dad threatened to "put me six feet under" with his fist up to my face during an argument at a holiday dinner. I remember keeping my head down in embarrassment and submission, and when I looked up from the table, everyone stayed silent. Some people cried, but no one helped me; no one stuck up for me or said one word to my dad. As I went to my car that night, his mother told me it was my fault he'd gotten so angry because I "frustrated" him. I knew that night, they were not my family. So, fuck no, they were not invited to my wedding.

I should have expected it from him, but I couldn't believe that two days before my wedding, he thought it was a good time to tell me how he really felt. He'd had 13 months, but instead he'd lied (as usual) and told me the opposite. Jen could tell something was up. She came over and I showed her the text.

She read it and rolled her eyes, annoyed I was letting him affect me.

"Hil, don't you dare let this man get to you right now. He wants you to be thinking about him because he knows you aren't, and that is why he sent that. Look around, this is your weekend. These are your people. You are about to marry the man of your dreams. He is not your family. There is a reason he's not here."

Jen was right. I picked up my phone and sent a reply. *"Sorry you and Grandma feel that way but we have spoken about this numerous times. You are not going to ruin my wedding day with your negativity. Thanks so much for your well wishes though!"*

41

SEPTEMBER 3, 2017—I DO!

Our wedding day was perfect. It rained a little bit, but it was fine. I do not believe the rain was good luck, though. I think people say that to make you feel better. Like when a bird shits on you—it definitely is not good luck; it just mentally makes the situation not as gross.

As he requested at our high school graduation, we invited our guidance counselor Chris Safina. It was a beautiful moment for the three of us when he showed up. Andrew and I had a sense of pride in showing him how far we both had come.

Every moment of our wedding was special, but five minutes I will never forget, were when Andrew and I exchanged vows. The only request I had for Andrew during the entire planning process was that it was important to me for us to write and read our own vows. I didn't want to say vows that everyone else said. We were different, we had overcome different obstacles, we were 29 and had known each other for over 15 years—I wanted this to be *our* moment.

Andrew read to me some of the kindest words I have ever heard. He thanked me for sticking by him, for never letting him fall, but not picking him up either since I knew he had to do that on his own. He told me that he admired me for my selflessness. That I love unconditionally and live with meaning, that I listen deeply and hear what people cannot put into words. He told me that he can't wait to wake up in the mornings with Cayman squeezed in between us. How I accept him for who he is and love him for who he is not. He told me it doesn't matter where we end up in life, because we would be together, and that waking up to me every day makes him feel like he can take on the world. He told me he couldn't wait for me to officially be his wife.

It was hard for me to keep it together.

In my vows to Andrew, I told him that I had been waiting for that day since I was 12 years old. I told him we had overcome more demons than most couples experience in a lifetime, but that everything we had conquered formed the incredible relationship we had right then. I told him I didn't care if it was raining out, because nothing could rain on that moment for me. I told him it had been my absolute pleasure watching him transform into the man he was. That he was a constant reminder and a beautiful example of how much power someone really has over their own life. I told him how much he has taught me about myself, about life, how proud I am of him, and how he inspires me every day to be a better person. I ended my vows by promising him I would never give him a hard time again about not taking me to prom; the wedding was enough to put that to rest.

Everyone started to laugh. It was a beautiful moment.

Our best man and matron of honor walked down the aisle hand-in-hand. Seeing his grandpa and my grandma together brought tears to our eyes. We have a picture of them walking down the aisle holding hands on our fireplace mantel now, and it is one of the most special pictures we will ever have.

By the end of the ceremony, the rain completely stopped and we danced the night away outside. The view of the beautiful lake was in front of us, and every time I looked at Andrew, I was overwhelmed with happiness and pride that we had made it to this day. To think he had almost died of a drug overdose just a few years earlier made this day more special than I can put into words. There are pictures of Andrew and me with him holding a water bottle; it was his way of not accidentally picking up someone's vodka-club. The "wine" in our Kiddush cup was grape juice. I love those pictures because they show how authentically "us" our wedding was.

After 15 years of waiting, Andrew was finally my husband.

42

HUSBAND AND WIFE

Andrew planned the most epic, amazing honeymoon for us for the following May. We spent almost three weeks traveling around Scandinavia. We went to Copenhagen, four cities in Norway, and two cities in Sweden. We ate at Michelin-starred restaurants nearly every day; we went to art museums and ate ice cream while walking down the streets of Stockholm. We took fjord cruises and spent a night in a Viking city that had a population of fewer than 100 people. There was not one drop of rain at any point in the trip, and we spent every day outside, exploring the world, enjoying the different food and cultures. It was incredible.

Post-wedding life with Andrew has been the best of the best of years. He found his passion again in the kitchen and went back to culinary school. When he eventually received the balance of the trust money from when his grandma passed away, he spent over $30,000 of it to pay off my student loans. I had never, ever received financial help my entire life. In one click of a button, Andrew wiped out debt that would have followed me for another 25 years. I was beyond grateful and emotional. He was so happy that he was finally in a position to help me, after years of me always helping him.

If I thought the first three years of his sobriety were good, I had no idea what I was in for. Andrew has become our household handyman, landscaper, finance manager, investor, garden expert, travel agent, librarian, and, my favorite—my personal chef. He encourages me to go out with my girlfriends and is my lifelong designated driver, waiting outside to pick my drunk ass up if I've had a few too many. He is responsible, dependable, honest, intelligent, thorough, resourceful, and creative. I trust him with every ounce of my soul and wouldn't want my life in anybody else's hands. Our relationship is deeper than best friends. We are soul mates. He just celebrated six years of sobriety, and I don't tell him enough how proud I am of him.

We still do not know if we want children. Although we've never really revisited the issue, it's something we still aren't ready for. The truth is, I have zero desire to be pregnant or push a baby out. On the other hand, I want to see the beautiful human that I know Andrew and I could create. I know we would both be great parents. But the idea of a baby is very different from the reality of a baby. And even though it is hard for society to accept the fact that as a woman I am just not sure yet, that is the truth. I do know, though, that whatever Andrew and I decide, we will decide together. And it will be the right decision for us.

I must say that I don't fully understand when people say marriage is hard. This year, Andrew and I celebrated 3 years of being married and 10 years of being together. Of course our relationship is not perfect, and like most wives, I have to tell him the same thing 400 times for him to remember. But marriage has been some of the easiest times of my life. We do not fight—ever. When we have disagreements or are not on the same page about something, it's because one of us is not communicating effectively. Since the night he told me he didn't want kids, we have never gone to bed angry at each other.

Maybe we got through all the hard shit before we got married, and because of how our relationship started and grew, these have been our golden years. I think if you have open communication, are honest about feelings, from big to small, and lead everything with love, it's easy.

For us, it's really easy.

43

WE FOUND A 51 PERCENT MATCH!

Andrew's 30th birthday was approaching in August of 2018, and I wanted to make the milestone extra special. I bought him a ton of gifts. One of them was a 23andMe genetics kit, since he had always been curious to find out more about his dad's side of the family. The company was having a buy-one-get-one-half-off sale, and since I was just as curious about my biological father's lineage and medical history, I bought myself a kit too.

Andrew and I sent in our tubes of spit and waited a few weeks for the results. Finally, I got an email that they were in. My heart was racing in excitement while I was anticipating finding out so much about my biological father. *Here we go! I wonder how interesting my results will be!* I opened up the email. . . .

"Hilary, you are 100% Ashkenazi Jewish."

I surveyed my computer screen in utter disappointment. This was not the climactic moment I was waiting for. *ARE YOU KIDDING ME? I waited weeks to find out I was 100 percent Jewish? This is total bullshit!*

Andrew's results said that he was 34 percent French and German, 33 percent British and Irish, 3 percent Scandinavian, and a few other things. That was pretty interesting. Me? Nope. One hundred percent Jewish. How riveting.

Before I logged off, I noticed there was an option that let you opt in to a "DNA share" program, which meant you were agreeing to let their software compare your DNA with that of anyone else who had opted in. I was frustrated with the experience and annoyed that I'd spent more than $100 to find out I was Jewish, which I already knew. To try to make the most of my investment, I figured what the hell and opted in to the DNA share. I told everyone that 23andMe was horrible and a waste of money. I was about to be proven wrong.

As the weeks went on, I forgot that I had opted in to the DNA share program. I figured I had received all the information available about C380—he was Jewish and that was that. I moved on with my life.

On October 10, 2018, almost nine years to the day after I'd received the sperm donor paperwork, I received an email from 23andMe that said, "Meet your DNA relatives." I was at work and didn't want to be bothered, thinking I would get some bullshit results like I'd gotten the first time. I had heard that most people got results connecting them with distant cousins, which I wasn't interested in.

I got home from work that night and Andrew wasn't home. I sat on the couch and opened my laptop. I clicked on the email to "meet my relatives." As soon as I logged on, a message popped up in the middle of my screen:

Hilary, we predict Jay Grossman is your Father.
You share 51.0% of your DNA with Jay.

My heart started palpitating. *Is this some kind of joke??* I peered around my basement apartment, waiting for someone to pop out of the closet with a video camera telling me I was being pranked. I glanced back at my screen and read it again.

Hilary, we predict Jay Grossman is your Father.

Holy shit! Holy shit! Holy shit! Holy shit! I packed a bowl and smoked a little weed, trying to calm down. I got up and peeked in my closets; no one was in there hiding. I logged off my account and then logged back in, thinking this was some kind of mistake. Same thing—*"You share 51.0% of your DNA with Jay. . . ."*

OH *MY GOD.*

I called Andrew. "Andrew, are you almost home?"

"Yeah, I'm pulling up. What's up?"

I hung up the phone.

Andrew came in the house and took one look at me. I clearly appeared frazzled. I told him what had happened and said he needed to log on to his account right away. I figured if 23andMe told him they'd found *his* dad, I'd know my results were total bullshit, since his dad had died 25 years earlier. *There is no way I spit into a tube and that was all it took to find my biological father.*

Andrew logged onto his account and started laughing. "Honey, my matches are only 1 to 2 percent. It says that they are distant cousins or something. Maybe this is really your dad!"

This made absolutely *no* sense to me. Why in the world would an anonymous sperm donor put his DNA out on a site like this? I logged back on to my account, still thinking this was a mistake.

Suddenly, I noticed that it listed three other matches:

Will H.: Half-brother, father's side. 20.7% DNA shared
Elizabeth D.: Half-sister, father's side. 27.1% DNA shared
Sabrina B.: Granddaughter. 24.5% DNA shared

WHAT?! HOW DO I HAVE A GRANDDAUGHTER?!

"This whole thing must be a scam. There is no way I have a grand-child!" I told Andrew.

I later learned that grandparents share approximately the same amount of DNA as half-siblings, but in the moment, I was looking for reasons not to believe my eyes. I started pacing back and forth. I snapped a picture of my screen and texted it to Jen. She immediately called me, freaking out.

"HIL . . . DID YOU JUST FIND YOUR DAD?!"

"Jen, I don't know. I don't know what is happening right now!" I said in a panic.

While on the phone with her, I googled Jay Grossman, and hundreds of people popped up.

"Jen, I am *never* going to find him. This is way too common a name."

"Hil, try searching 'Jay Grossman dentist.' His sperm donor application said he was going to school for dentistry; maybe he finished and became one!"

Great idea, Jen, why didn't I think of that? I took her advice and nervously clicked "search." Suddenly, a tall, handsome man popped up, listed as a concierge dentist in Brentwood, California. There was only *one* "Jay Grossman dentist."

Jen did the same search from her computer for "Jay Grossman dentist." After a few seconds of silence she shrieked, "Oh my God, Hil, you look *just* like him. This is definitely your dad!"

I didn't think I looked much like this man, but Jen was adamant that he was my father. She kept saying, "You have the same nose! The same chin! The same mouth! How can you not see this right now?"

Everything was happening so fast, it was too much for me to handle at that moment.

"Jen, I don't know what is happening right now. I think maybe we just found him. I have to go. I'll call you later."

I hung up the phone and started investigating this random dentist in depth. There were hundreds of videos of him online. There were pictures of him in his office, as well as videos of him speaking on TV shows like *The Doctors* and *Dr. Phil*, and on CNN as a "dental expert." There were pictures of him with Jay Leno, John Travolta, William H. Macy (who was one of my favorite actors from *Shameless*), and Sharon Stone.

I started laughing hysterically. *Yeah, right, this guy is my dad!* Then I came across a picture that said, "Sending our best wishes and appreciation to Homeless not Toothless, Love Michelle Obama"—with a picture of the Obama family and a little insert of this random Jay Grossman on the photo. *This definitely cannot be him. I know for sure whoever my biological father is, that he does NOT know the Obamas.*

Although I felt certain this man was not my father, I was still intrigued, since he seemed like such an interesting character. I went onto Facebook and searched "Jay Grossman." Again, a ton of people popped up. I came across a profile that looked just like the guy I had been googling, so for kicks, I clicked on the profile.

This guy was super handsome. He had a beautiful family—two sons and a daughter. His wife looked so sweet, you could tell she was a caring person as soon as you saw her. On this Jay Grossman's Facebook page, he was tagged by "The Best of Los Angeles Awards" account in a photo that had the caption "Celebrity dentist Dr. Jay Grossman spotted drinking coffee at a local café." *Celebrity dentist? Spotted drinking coffee? Who the hell is this guy?*

I continued to look at his profile, and as I did, my stomach felt like an Olympic gymnast was doing a floor routine inside of it. His "about me" section read as follows:

- *Cosmetic Dentist at Concierge Dentist*
- *Dentistry Professor at NYU College of Dentistry*
- *Executive Director at Homeless Not Toothless*
- *Former LT US Navy*
- *Studied at NYU*
- *Studied at SUNY Albany*
- *Went to John F. Kennedy, Plainview, NY*
- *Lives in Los Angeles, California*
- *From Plainview, New York*
- *Married to Briar Flicker Grossman*

I could *not* believe what I was reading. This man went to SUNY Albany; so did I. He was from Plainview, which was about 12 minutes from where I grew up. He went to New York University, which meant he was in New York in his early 20s, which is when my biological father donated sperm. Then I clicked on "Homeless Not Toothless" and saw that he ran a charity that provided free dental care to homeless veterans, foster children, and other underprivileged groups. This was the charity noted on the picture with Michelle Obama. *This man runs a charity? Seriously?! Who is he?*

Honestly, the second I saw the charity, in my gut I thought maybe it could be him, my biological father. My whole life I had been so passionate about charity work, I'd write business plans for charities, I was passionate about volunteering. It *would* make sense if it ran through my bones. I still didn't want to believe it, though. This guy seemed too extraordinary to be my dad.

I had no idea what to do at this moment. There was no way to be certain this Jay was the same Jay I was matched with on 23andMe, so I told myself not to get ahead of myself. I decided not to call my mom or anyone and to just sleep on it. I needed to get my thoughts together.

I tried to sleep. That didn't work out so well.

44

ARE YOU MY BROTHER?

I could not sleep at all that night. I kept thinking, *Did I really just find my biological father? No. It can't be him. He looks too . . . normal?*

I guess I'd never really thought about what my biological father would be like (aside from a drug lord), since I was always told I'd never find him. I hadn't allowed myself to get caught up in the fantasy of him, so I hadn't prepared myself for this possibility. That morning while I was getting ready for work, I called my mom.

"Mom, 23andMe found a 51 percent match, and it says it's my dad. I found a Facebook profile for a dentist with his name, but I'm not sure if it's him. He seems too famous. But he grew up in New York, went to Albany, and runs a charity. It also says I have two half-siblings and a granddaughter."

My mom was silent at first, settling into her complete shock at this random yet fascinating news.

Then her responses were (1) "Why would he have given you 51 percent of your DNA? If anything, I gave you more of my DNA." (2) "Holy shit, he lived in New York and went to the same college as you?" And (3) "Honey, if he runs a charity—it really may be him. It makes sense if it's in your blood."

I thought it was funny my mom was pissed that this man possibly gave me 2 percent more of my DNA than she did. But it was very important to me that she and Brock were comfortable with me trying to find out more about these people. Both of them were really happy for me and thought I should continue trying to contact these newly found relatives. With their blessings, I felt way more comfortable digging deeper. I didn't want to offend either of them, so it meant the world to me that they were supportive.

I hung up the phone and couldn't wait any longer. Now that my mom had told me she was okay with me seeing where this journey would take me, I logged back on to my computer. 23andMe had a messaging app, so I sent a message to this random man, Jay Grossman.

"Hi Jay, my name is Hilary. It is nice to 'meet' you. I was wondering if you saw the DNA match between us. Let me know if you'd like to speak further. I'm looking forward to it."

Andrew told me to go to work and try to focus. *Easy for you to say!* I got to work 20 minutes later and immediately logged on to 23andMe. No response from Jay. I kept the window open on my screen and would refresh it every half hour. . . . Nothing.

What kind of sick man signs up as an anonymous sperm donor and then puts his DNA out in public like this, only to ignore me? He must be a real asshole.

The reality was, only a short time had passed since I'd messaged him, but I was looking for reasons to make him a "bad guy." Plus, if it *was* the Jay in the Facebook profile I had found, he lived in California and it was 5 a.m. when I sent him the message. Still, I told myself he was a jerk for not getting back to me instantly.

I tried to get through the rest of my workday acting normal. By this time Andrew and I had moved off Long Island and I'd been at a new job for only three months. None of my coworkers knew anything about me. I could not start telling them about my crazy night's events without telling them 15 years of dramatic history.

I waited impatiently for five o'clock and then sped home. I logged back on to 23andMe—NOTHING! *What a dick this guy is.*

I poked around on the website for a while and then figured I'd try another route. Will, the half-brother it said I had, had a picture on his profile. He looked about my age and looked just like the Jay I had been investigating on Facebook. I figured I had nothing to lose. I sent Will a message.

"Hi Will, nice to 'meet' you! Was wondering if you saw our DNA match. . . . Let me know if you'd like to chat!"

Within minutes, I had a message in my inbox. The gymnast was back at her floor routine in my belly.

"Hi Hilary! I had not seen our match. It looks like you may be in for the same adventure I've recently embarked on? I'm absolutely happy to chat. Let me know if you'd prefer a different interface than this one?"

My heart started racing faster than it did the night before. *The same adventure? Is this guy really my brother?!* I thought I was going to have a heart attack. I guess I'd never thought about what I would do if these people answered me. And now, Will had answered me! *What am I going to do now?*

Within two minutes, Will emailed me saying if I was comfortable sharing, he wanted to hear my story. I took a deep breath, trying to keep myself calm. I did my best to sum up my story, essentially telling Will I had known since I was 20 that my dad wasn't my biological father, and I had done 23andMe to find out more about my biological father's medical history. I told him I knew I was a sperm donor baby and had a copy of the donor's application but had been told I would never find my father due to anonymity laws. I said 23andMe had matched up Jay Grossman as my father and Will as my brother, and had also found a sister and a granddaughter. Then I asked him to tell me a little bit about himself and his story.

Will sent me another email. An email that put me into my next Forever Haze of After.

45

HOLY SHIT!! I FOUND HIM!!

Wow. Very interesting, and as I think you're going to find, very common!

I am 30 as well. I knew my dad wasn't my dad from a fairly young age . . . around 8–10, I can't remember exactly. . . . I'm married, have two daughters, and have always been curious about my ancestry. My dad passed away about a year and a half ago and I decided to take a test to figure out some of that stuff, and I ended up right where you are.

What I will tell you is that you have more than one other half-sister. There is Liz (32) in NY (who you mentioned), Sabrina (29) in Toronto, and Jordan (31/girl) in Arizona. All of their stories are VERY similar to yours. (I'm in Kansas City, by the way.) I'd be happy to make introductions to them if you'd like that?

Jay, our dad, lives in California. As of now, Liz, Jordan, and I have all met him. I'd be happy to make an introduction, if that's something you'd like. He's really quite a nice guy, and his whole family has been exceptionally cool with this entire . . . situation? Hahaha. Jay has 3 kids, Sydney (29), Eric (27), and Ari (21).

Whew, okay, there's a lot more to share, but back at ya!
—Will

Nothing in life can prepare you for an email like this. It was 10:30 p.m. when I received this message, which catapulted me into my next "after." Andrew was fast asleep. I shot out of bed and was pacing around my apartment like a madwoman. I read this email over and over and over again, trying to process every single word.

Imagine lying in your bed at 30 years old and finding out you have three sisters and a brother, spread across the continent, who have all recently located *your* biological father, whom you've been trying to find for a decade. At the end of the email Will gave me his cell phone number and said he understood this was a lot for me to take in and if I wanted to call or text him, I could.

I reread the part about Jay. "Jay, *our* dad . . ." *What the fuck. OUR dad? It's MY dad? It's OUR dad?* I couldn't fully comprehend what I was reading. He ". . . lives in California?" Then it dawned on me.

HOLY SHIT!! I FOUND HIM!!

I went back onto Facebook and took a screenshot of the guy in the profile I had found the night before. I texted the number Will had given me.

"Will, it's Hil. Is this the man you are saying is my dad?" I included the picture of Jay.

To be clear, that was the strangest text message I have ever sent anyone.

"Yup! That's our dad!" Will replied with a wink emoji.

I stopped in my tracks, nearly dropping my phone from fainting. *Holy shit. That is really my dad? My dad is a celebrity dentist? He grew up in New York and now has a family in LA? He runs a charity? He goes on TV? Michelle Obama wishes him happy holidays?!* A hundred million things were running through my mind at once. I was overwhelmed.

Andrew was sleeping, and I needed to speak to someone who could focus and listen to me. *Who am I going to call? Who could understand what I am feeling right now?* Well, I had just found out there were actually four people who could understand. . . .

Will sent me another text, almost as if he'd heard what my brain was saying. "Listen, I know this is a lot for you to take in. Please don't feel weird if you want to call me to talk to someone. We are siblings, ya know?"

I read his text a few times. *SIBLINGS?! What the hell! Why is he being so nice to me?!* I looked at Andrew; he was snoring. I really needed to talk to someone. I felt weird about it, but hey, he offered. I went outside and called Will.

The sweetest guy answered the phone. He had a strong Midwestern accent to me, definitely not a New Yorker! You would think it would have been awkward at first, but it wasn't at all. It was kind of like we were old friends catching up after years of not seeing each other. I thanked Will for speaking to me and helping me through my crazy night. He explained that they had "all gone through this," referring to the nights that each of my newfound siblings had found Jay themselves.

Will was happy he could be there for me. I asked him about his family and his daughters. He pointed out to me that I have nieces! It was shocking to hear, but super cute. He told me that all my new biological siblings had done 23andMe within the past six months, so the situation was fairly new to everyone. It's funny that all five of us were between 29 and 32 years old and had each known for various amounts of time that our dads were not our dads, but all somehow had done the test within a few months of each other. Maybe something in our DNA had told us to do it around the same time.

Will pointed out that not only were he, Liz, Sabrina, and Jordan my siblings, but Jay's three kids were *also* my siblings, which for some reason I hadn't realized initially. *OH MY GOD! I JUST WENT FROM HAVING ONE BROTHER TO SEVEN ADDITIONAL SIBLINGS IN UNDER AN HOUR!*

I asked Will how he had first connected and spoken with Jay, since Jay wasn't answering his 23andMe messages. Will's story was so random and nuts, it was almost too crazy for me to believe. But it is true, and it's essentially the reason my story ended up the way it did.

When Will was matched up with Jay on 23andMe, he did some research but, like me, did not think the famous dentist popping up on

Google was actually his dad. After not getting a response through the messenger on 23andMe, Will found Jay's Facebook profile, which had a picture of Jay at 19 years old in which he looked identical to Will at that age. Will knew right away it had to be his dad. After some impressive detective work, he noticed that his sister-in-law and Jay's sister-in-law had a mutual friend—a poodle breeder in Missouri, of all things. After some back-and-forth, the breeder contacted Jay's sister-in-law to get him in touch with Will. Jay's sister-in-law then reached out to Jay and his wife, Briar, thinking this was a mistake, since no one even knew Jay had been a sperm donor. When Jay was told to check his 23andMe account, that was when and how he found out he had more biological children: Will, Sabrina, and Liz.

Special shout-out to this poodle breeder in Missouri. If that isn't fate at its finest, I don't know what is.

Will is a successful architect who manages projects worldwide for new stadiums that are being built. In the years leading up to when he found Jay, he spent two years traveling bimonthly to California for a new project. He would dine at restaurants within a half mile of Jay's office, never knowing his biological father was within walking distance.

Will told me about his trip to California to meet Jay and the family, which happened a month or so after he and Jay first spoke. Even though Will had told me in his email that he, Liz, and Jordan had already met Jay, I still could not comprehend that Jay *wanted* to know us. *Why? What could he want from us? This makes no sense!*

Will answered all my questions but told me that Jay would be happy to answer them as well. He assured me that Jay was not ignoring me and would be happy to speak to me. Will said he would contact the rest of the group in the morning to tell them about me, if I was interested in that. I told Will I did want him to reach out to Jay and pass along my contact info to the rest of the BioSibs. (This was the word we would all later coin to label our relationship. We are biological siblings. We are BioSibs.)

Before we hung up, I couldn't stop thanking Will for speaking to me and helping me through this night. This stranger had told me more information about myself in one hour than I had been able to find out in 10 years.

My journey with them was just beginning.

46
"WELCOME TO THE BIOFAMILY!"

I tossed and turned that entire night. I was on information overload after my conversation with Will. I kept thinking, *I can't believe Jay wants to talk to me. Why would he want to talk to me?* I never in a million years thought I would find him, and if I did find him, I never thought he would want to know anything about me.

The next morning I got up and told Andrew about my night's events. He could not believe what I was telling him. I called my mom to tell her about my conversation as well, and she, again, was in shock. She couldn't believe I had found four other sperm-donor siblings and that Jay had already met three of them. I couldn't believe it either.

That morning I got to work, again trying to remain cool. Within minutes of sitting down at my desk, my email started blowing up. "WELCOME TO THE BIOFAMILY!" was the subject line. I had individual emails from Sabrina, Liz, and Jordan—my SISTERS?! They were all so sweet and welcoming. I wanted to talk to them and could not focus at work.

I barely knew my boss, since I had only been with the company for a few months, but I walked into her office and told her I had to speak to her privately. I closed the door.

"I know this is going to sound weird, but two nights ago I randomly found my biological father and seven siblings. They are all emailing me right now for the first time, and I need a moment to get myself together. Is it okay if I take an early lunch break and leave the office?" It wasn't even 10 a.m.

My boss looked back at me stunned. "That is one of the most interesting things an employee has ever said to me. Take as much time as you need."

I left the office and jumped into my car. I drove to a random parking lot and sat there with a notebook. I read all my BioSibs' emails multiple times and tried to take notes. Everyone had such interesting and amazing stories, but it was hard to remember all the details. These girls poured their hearts out to me. I didn't receive one-or-two-sentence emails; they were long and in-depth, telling me their life stories and what had brought each of them to that exact moment in time.

———

As I read my sisters' emails, I felt the same way I did when I spoke to Will on the phone—like we were old friends catching up. It was fascinating to me that I didn't know these people, but they had all felt the exact same way I was feeling. Before I read their emails, I looked them up on Facebook so I could at least know what my sisters looked like. They were helping me through this unusual situation and welcomed me with open arms, so I wanted to put faces to names. It felt too good to be true, but it wasn't. It was real.

Liz is a fellow Long Islander and grew up 10 miles away from me. It was crazy to me that my half-sister had lived so close to me my whole life and we never knew it. Our high schools played each other in sports! To think that we could have been at the same place at the same time was mind-blowing. Liz and I connected in the sense that she too did not have a relationship with her dad, and after her mom lost her battle with cancer, she found out her dad was not her biological father. She wanted to learn more about her medical history, so she took the Ancestry.com test, which matched her up with Sabrina. They were originally matched as cousins, but after speaking, they realized they were actually sisters. Months after we connected, Liz was "coincidentally" filming a TV series across the street from the building where I now worked, and I got a chance to stop by. If it hadn't been for 23andMe, my sister would have been across the street from me and I would never have known it.

Sabrina is the only BioSib (so far) from Canada, but aside from that and her being almost a foot taller than me, she reminds me of myself! We have similar personalities and attitudes, we grew up alike, and we were both responsibly rebellious as teenagers. Sabrina's journey with Jay was unlike the rest of ours, though. Whereas we were all eager to meet Jay, Sabrina wasn't even comfortable speaking to him because she felt guilty about her dad, who was in the final stages of his life when she found Jay. She and her dad had an incredibly close relationship, and he battled kidney, heart and lung disease for years. Sabrina found out he wasn't her biological father after she secretly went to a doctor when she was 16 to get tested to donate a kidney to him. When she told me she'd gone through that alone, it showed me how strong and courageous a woman she was, even at just 16 years old—and I was proud to be her BioSister.

A few days after the test, the doctor called her back to the office to discuss the test results. At 16 years old in Canada, you are considered a legal adult and can see a doctor without parental supervision. This was when the doctor told her that not only was she not a transplant match for her dad, but they weren't a genetic match either. Sabrina told me she didn't say a word to her parents about this and assumed the doctors were somehow wrong. It wasn't until five years later that her dad randomly told her during dinner one night that he had a vasectomy before marrying Sabrina's mom, so they had opted for a sperm donor. It wasn't until he sadly lost his battle and passed that she was ready to meet Jay.

Jordan and I easily have the most notable physical similarities. When I saw a picture of her, it was obvious we were related. We are the same height, have the same hair and eye colors, and walk exactly the same. We compared pictures of us at four years old, and people could have thought we were twins. 23andMe has us sharing the most DNA, at 30.3 percent, which is pretty high for half-siblings. Jordan was born in Kansas City and was conceived in the same hospital as Will—I know, how nuts. Even crazier, Jordan and Will are both architects. We joke that they were in the same "donation" from Jay due to their similarities. Sort of gross, but definitely true. If Jordan had never moved out of KC, she would have attended the same local architectural school that Will went to, and they would have been only a year apart.

Jordan was always interested in genealogy and did the Ancestry.com test after she received it as a present. Her parents split up when she was younger and her mom moved her out to Phoenix, but Jordan remained close with her dad. Aside from his being in his 50s when she was born, there was no indication that he wasn't her dad. When her mom found out she had done the DNA test, she decided to tell Jordan the truth about her being a sperm-donor baby. Like Sabrina's dad, Jordan's dad had had a vasectomy before marrying her mom. In the same week that Jordan found out her dad was not her dad, she located Jay, her biological father.

———

My sisters and I exchanged numbers and they added me to the "BioSib group text," which was hysterical as we all shared different traits to see if they "ran in the family." We figured out that most of us were flat-footed and Jay had passed that down to us. (Thanks, Jay.)

After some time, I went back to my office. I was on cloud nine, feeling like I had just formed relationships with people who would be a part of my life forever. Just as I was getting back into work mode, I received an email from 23andMe that said I had a private message.

"Jay Grossman sent you a message: Hi Hilary! Elizabeth texted me this morning, so I logged on and saw your match. I am happy to speak with you! My number is . . . Feel free to call me today!"

My heart was convulsing. *HOLY SHIT, MY DAD JUST SENT ME A*

MESSAGE! IT'S REALLY HIM! I went out into the hallway and started walking in circles. *I can't call him today, I'm not ready!* You'd think that after speaking to my siblings I'd be ready, but I wasn't. Talking to them was different from the reality of talking to my father for the first time. I don't know why I thought I would ever be ready for a moment like this, but I wasn't.

I texted my BioSibs. "Guys, Oh My God. Jay just messaged me and he wants me to call him—*today!* What do I do?"

My new siblings coached me through this moment. They understood how nervous I was, since they all had experienced the exact same emotions when Jay first reached out to them. They assured me how amazing Jay was and how it was normal for me to feel what I was feeling. I had never met them, I'd only found out about them two days before, but if I hadn't had them to help me through this, I don't know how I would have gotten through it.

I decided I needed a couple of days to mentally prepare to speak to my biological father for the first time. I texted Jay and introduced myself. It was a Friday afternoon, but I asked him if he'd be available that Sunday. He replied immediately, "Absolutely! I'll call you at 3 p.m. your time!"

Ready or not, the time was set. I couldn't believe I was texting with my father.

47

"HI, HILARY! IT'S JAY!"

I was a basket of emotions that weekend. It probably would have been easier if I had just spoken to Jay that Friday and gotten it over with. Instead, I drowned in anxiety for two days leading up to the call.

Sunday came around and I told Andrew I couldn't do anything at all that day. I paced around my apartment for hours, waiting for 3 p.m. to arrive. My BioSibs were texting me, "Hil, don't worry, it's going to be fine, we promise!" It was reassuring to have people to help me who had been through exactly what I was going through.

Three o'clock came and right on the nose, my phone started ringing. "Jay Grossman is calling." My heart was pounding, like there was a marching band trapped inside my body. It felt like I waited hours before I answered. I was taking deep breaths, trying to calm down. *Don't freak out, it's just your biological father calling. No big deal.* I picked up the phone.

"Hi, Hilary! It's Jay!"

Oh my God. It's him.

Jay was kind and outgoing. He took the lead in the conversation, likely feeling my hesitation and nerves. By now, he had his speech down to a science. I was the fifth child who had found him in six months, so he had practiced this conversation before. He asked me

196

questions about my life and my parents, and if I had any siblings. I told him I had a brother and he casually said, "Cool! Am I his dad too?" He seemed kind of bummed he wasn't Brock's dad! He told me he had a spreadsheet of all my BioSibs' information so he could keep track. Now I know where I got that trait from. . . .

I asked Jay why he had donated sperm in the first place. He explained that NYU was expensive and his parents didn't have a lot of money—something I related to. While he was at school one day in the mid-'80s, doctors came into his class and said there was a new procedure available called artificial insemination. This process was originally geared to help people who had come home from the war have families, since so many returned infertile from injuries or chemical warfare. The doctors said they would pay well for anyone who donated and the only requirements at that time were that you needed to have a high IQ and had to be HIV negative. In hopes of making some extra money to put toward school, and to be able to pay for a dinner or two for his girlfriend (now his wife, Briar), he donated, since he met the criteria.

It's funny that after I'd received a copy of his donor application nearly 10 years prior, I had inferred that he was donating sperm to help pay for med school. I was right.

Jay asked me if I had any questions for him, and I did. I had been waiting to ask him questions for 10 years! First, I asked him if he had any medical conditions or anything I had to worry about. He said this was the first question all my BioSibs had asked him as well. His response was, "I have every hair on my head, I don't take any pills, I'm 55 years old and exercise four times a week. I have no medical conditions and I try to be a good man. You have no excuse to be an asshole."

I thought his humor was funny. *I guess he isn't the drug lord that I imagined. . . .*

I asked Jay how his wife and children felt about this whole "situation." He appreciated that I asked about them, and he told me they were really excited for us. He said that his wife, Briar, remembered when he donated sperm and she had always wanted a big family. She embraced my other BioSibs in a very maternal way and was looking forward to speaking to me, if I was interested. Jay said that Briar had a doctorate in psychology and specialized in psychoanalytic psychotherapy. *Oh perfect, because I could definitely use the help of a shrink right now.*

Jay shared with me that his daughter Sydney and her wife, Brit, had announced that they'd successfully conceived via a sperm donor the day before Will found Jay. In 24 hours, Jay found out he would be a grandfather thanks to a sperm donor, and that he had a biological son from his own sperm donations nearly 30 years prior. Talk about unbelievable timing.

I asked Jay why he had done 23andMe in the first place and if it was to find any of us kids. He honestly told me no, and that he had actually forgotten he'd donated sperm. He said, "Please do not take this the wrong way, but I donated strictly for the money at the time. When I did the DNA test a few years ago, I didn't even think about it! I was doing it because I wanted to learn more about my lineage. I never thought about potentially having other children."

I was okay with this response and appreciated his honesty. Finally, a dad in my life was being honest. He wasn't trying to sugarcoat anything. He found out about us and embraced us—that was what mattered.

Jay and I were on the phone for over an hour. As the minutes passed, it became easier for me to let my guard down. He told me about the charity he founded in 1992 and how he got started with his career. He told me that Sharon Stone was on the board and since inception, they have provided more than $5 million in free dental care to the homeless. I was astonished by the kindness in this man's heart.

I asked Jay why he wanted to know us. Although I was happy, I was confused. Why would he be so willing to open his life to the BioSibs and me? Why would he want this "baggage"?

He seemed equally confused about my question. "What do you mean? I'm your father. Of course I want to know you. Lucky for me I got to skip over the expensive college part." He laughed.

I laughed too. *Don't worry, Jay, I paid for my own college, but I'll get to that another time*, I thought. His words echoed in my head. "I'm your father. . . ." *How crazy is this?*

We laughed about the similarities between us. How he grew up just a few minutes from where I grew up. How we both went to college at SUNY Albany. How he came from a humble beginning, his family didn't have any money, and they struggled like my mom and I did. He asked me if I flossed every night and scolded me when I told him I did not. Typical dentist.

While wrapping up the call, he told me that his youngest son, my youngest brother, Ari, was currently in New York City attending college to be an actor (just like Liz). He told me that he and Briar were coming in the following month to see Ari in a play and asked if Andrew and I would want to spend the weekend with them.

Jay had made me feel so comfortable through this conversation, and knowing that three of my other BioSibs had already met him, I actually couldn't *wait* to see this guy in person. Jay gave me the dates of their visit and told me to keep my calendar clear. He said he was so excited to meet me and spend time together.

I hung up the phone in a daze. I couldn't believe *this* was my father.

48

"DON'T BE NERVOUS, WE'RE JUST ON THE WAY TO MEET YOUR DAD!"

After speaking to Jay, I felt like my world was rocked. For so long, I had imagined what kind of man he would be. For years, I'd say to my grandma, "I just hope he's a good guy!" Now I knew that he was. It was crazy to tell my friends and family that not only had I found him, but I'd spoken to him, *and* that he wanted to meet me. People could not believe he wanted to be a part of my life.

For the weeks leading up to my first meetup with Jay, we kept in touch regularly. By then, I had spoken to Briar and Jay's kids through texts and calls and felt like I had known them forever. The weirdest part about the whole situation was how *not* weird it was.

My BioSib Liz, my fellow Long Islander, planned to join us the weekend Jay and Briar were in town. It was hard for me to grasp that I'd be meeting my biological father, a sister, and a brother all in one weekend. I was nervous but excited.

Amanda remained one of my best friends from college and lent me her apartment in the city for the weekend, since she was going out of town. While Andrew and I were getting ready to meet Jay for lunch, I was quiet. Although I felt comfortable speaking to him on the phone, meeting him was a different ballgame. It was hard for me to say anything because my mind was full of "what-ifs" and all the things that could go wrong. *What if he doesn't like me? What if he is actually not a nice guy? What if I'm too poor for him? What if his wife and son hate me?* I was in my own head.

We got into the cab and Andrew looked at me. "Honey, don't be nervous. We're just on the way to meet your dad!" he joked, trying to lighten up the mood.

By the time we arrived at the hotel, I thought I was going to throw up. I was a bag of nerves. It was hitting me that within seconds, I would be seeing the man that made me. Even though I didn't know him, he *was* my father. Andrew told me to relax and assured me that everything was going to be okay. My BioSibs were texting me: "Have so much fun! You are going to love Jay and Briar!"

I walked into the restaurant and immediately laid eyes on Jay. His eyes had a glimmer in them, and his diamond stud earring was sparkling around the room. I was doing breathing exercises while I walked up to him, trying to make sure I didn't pass out on the way. Jay looked up from the table and started smiling ear to ear. He got up and walked over to me and gave me a big, long hug.

Hmmmm, a hug? This is weird. I hadn't received physical affection like that from my other dad in over 20 years. Jay's hug made me feel so protected, immediately. It was a comforting feeling that I was not used to. He told me he was so thrilled to finally meet me. Tears filled my eyes. I couldn't believe *this* was my dad.

Jay's wife, Briar, was one of the kindest souls I've ever met. My BioSibs and I credit Briar for allowing these relationships to grow. The reality is, if Jay had found us and Briar had had a problem with it, Jay probably would not have moved forward in pursuing relationships with us. We weren't even sure why Briar wanted to be a part of our lives, but she did. She really, really did.

Sitting down with my biological father for the first time was an out-of-body experience. Thank God I had Andrew there with me to make me more comfortable. Every time I looked at Jay, I couldn't believe I was really sitting down with him. For 10 years, he was C380 —now I was seeing him in the flesh. Now he wasn't just a donor code; he was right in front of me.

Jay and Briar asked me questions about my life and my relationship with my other dad. I told them some of the good times and many of the bad times. I told Jay how I had tried to get information from the sperm bank but they'd told me I would never find him. I told him the things his donor application said, like how he was going to school for dentistry and played the saxophone.

Briar chimed in, "What? You played the saxophone?" she asked while giggling.

Maybe Jay fibbed a little on the application! At least that lie was better than my guess that he was a drug lord pretending to go to dental school.

I told them about the conversation I had with my mom when she finally revealed to me the "20-year secret." When I looked at Jay, he had tears streaming down his face. I couldn't believe how much he cared. He really, honestly cared.

While we were eating lunch, Ari showed up to say hi before his play. I couldn't believe I was now meeting my youngest brother! Ari was super handsome and enjoyed making fun of my "Lawng Eye-land" accent the entire time. He was taking a class on dialects and accents and pulled out his notebook to prove to me that I talked like a "text-book New Yorker."

Once we stopped laughing, I told Ari that I really appreciated how open he was being about me and the rest of the BioSibs meeting Jay and his family.

Ari replied, "It's not like my dad had affairs with all of your moms. It doesn't surprise me he was a sperm donor; he always does stuff like this. Just like when a homeless guy lived with us for two years. Nothing surprises me with my dad anymore."

I appreciated his viewpoint. I guess he was right—it wasn't like Jay had done anything hurtful to his family. He had donated sperm nearly 30 years before this. But it was still cool that they were being so open toward us and had such an amazing perspective about the whole thing. I was intrigued about the homeless man living with them, though. . . .

Jay proceeded to tell me that years ago, he had hired one of his homeless patients to do some construction work at his house after the patient, who I'll call Jeff, said he had "done construction work for Sharon Stone." Even though Jay didn't believe him, he was trying to give this guy a break.

The story goes that Jeff showed up to work on time and was a very detailed, hard worker. The next day he was back early to continue. Jay lives in a high-end neighborhood, and his neighbors were complaining about a homeless man sleeping in a beat-up car on the street. It turns out, Jeff didn't have a place to sleep and was camping out in his car to make sure he got to Jay's on time.

When Jay and Briar found out that Jeff was sleeping in his car, they gave him an ultimatum. They told him that he could either sleep in their spare bedroom and finish the job, or he was fired. That invitation changed Jeff's life. He ended up staying with them for two years, started working, and got his life back on track—all due to the kindness of Jay and Briar.

A few months later, Jay's phone rang and it was Sharon Stone. Sharon was interested in Jay's charity and thought that they could partner up. When Jay asked her how she had gotten his information, she responded, "Jeff gave it to me!" Jeff hadn't been lying after all. Thanks to this homeless man, Jay and Sharon teamed up and have helped treat more than 60,000 homeless people and others from underprivileged groups. Talk about fate.

I listened to this story in awe that this kind, philanthropic, gentle soul was my father. I felt so proud and relieved that I was a product of him.

It was a humbling moment for me. To think back 10 years prior, when I found out my dad was not my dad, I felt relieved. Fast-forward to this day, finally meeting the man who actually made me. I was relieved again.

We spent the entire weekend laughing and talking, trying to catch up on 30 years of missed history. Jay was interested in how my mom felt about the whole situation and was elated to hear she was support-ive. Jay told me he hoped to meet her one day. I thought about how special that moment could be and wished it would happen.

The next day Liz came and met us for lunch. Meeting my sister was amazing. We had a lot of similarities but didn't look alike at all. We couldn't get over that we had lived so close to each other our whole lives and hadn't known it. We bonded over the fact that both of us were estranged from our dads and how amazing it was for us to find out our biological father was a man like Jay.

When the weekend came to a close, I was upset that my time with Jay and Briar was ending. It was such a strange feeling to meet your father at 30 years old. So many of my questions had been answered. It was fascinating to me that even though Jay was wealthy and successful, without hesitation he opened his life up to us—never thinking once that we had ill intentions or wanted to know him for financial gain or anything of the sort. I didn't even really know him, but I admired him.

Andrew and I got back to our apartment, and I was in amazement at my experiences over the last two days. I sent Jay a text.

"Jay, I am still on cloud nine from this weekend. It was such an absolute pleasure to meet you and of course Briar and Ari. I have such a feeling of relief and comfort knowing you are my biological father. I am really proud to be a part of you. Thank you so much for opening your life up to me."

A few minutes later I got a reply.

"Right back at you, it was a pleasure for us as well. Imagine the excitement and joy of seeing my DNA being beautiful, happy, healthy and in a committed relationship. What else could a father ask for? I look forward to our continued growth."

49

MY FOREVER HAZE OF: MEETING JAY

I knew the moment I met Jay, my life was forever changed. Seeing his kindness and compassion allowed me to let go of all the preconceptions I had made up about my biological father.

Jay could not have been more opposite to my dad. Whereas my dad never knew how to love or care for me, it was in Jay's nature. Whereas my dad never hugged me or showed me affection, Jay squeezed me close. Where my dad never kept a job, Jay was a successful entrepreneur with numerous companies and patented products. Where my dad never gave a dime to help me, Jay made it his life's work and passion to help people in need.

The first time I spoke to Jay, he told me I had "no excuse to be an asshole." This couldn't have been truer. Between having my mom as my mom and Jay as my biological father, I hit the jackpot. Knowing they both are my parents gives me drive and inspiration to be a good person every single day.

After I met Jay, I let go of any remaining threads of anger I had toward my dad. When I reflect back on my childhood, I realize that I wanted him to be something he wasn't. I wanted to have a dad so badly, someone I could call for advice and laugh with. I never had that. Now, I don't need him to act like a dad. I actually don't need anything from him. Once I realized that, I couldn't be angry anymore. There wasn't anything left to be angry about. I never told him I'd found Jay. In fact, I haven't told my dad about anything special that has happened in my life—maybe because I didn't want to give him the opportunity to ruin those things. When I recently found out my dad was dying of cancer, I realized that if I had never found Jay, I might not have been able to allow myself to tell my dad I don't hate him. I might not have been able to give him the courtesy of letting him die in peace. Thanks to Jay, I was able to do so.

I recently had an opportunity to go to California and stay with Jay and Briar. Six of my BioSibs were there, and it's always so special to be with them. During my trip, Jay took me to a charity event he was hosting that weekend. He knows how interested I am in the charity; we've had numerous conversations about how my dream job would be to run an East Coast division. I spent the day signing in UCLA students and taking pictures for social media. As the event was wrapping up, I watched interviews of the homeless patients speaking about their experiences that day. It was emotional for me to see these people cry in appreciation of what Jay does for them. Jay's high-end lifestyle is something I am not used to, but to me, his philanthropic side is the most impressive part of him. It was incredibly humbling to see that side of him, to see the extreme differences between him and my other dad.

Jay has been able to answer all the questions I formed over the years. In one swoop, 10 years' worth of worry and anxiety disappeared. Knowing who he was gave me an overwhelming sense of fulfillment and wholeness.

Jay was the missing piece to my puzzle.

50

"WE HAVE ANOTHER BROTHER!"

In early 2019, Jay shared the news that he was being honored with the Harry Strusser Award at the NYU graduation ceremony for his extraordinary humanitarian efforts with the homeless population. This was a huge deal. Jay's family would be in New York for a few days, and he invited all the BioSibs to attend. There was no chance in hell I was missing this.

Two months before the ceremony, Sydney and her wife, Brit, were watching a show about three identical twins who were separated at birth and found each other later in life. Out of curiosity, Brit hopped onto Jay's 23andMe account and couldn't believe her eyes. She saw that Jay had another match—which meant we had another sibling.

Brit and Sydney sent a message out to our group chat: "HOLY SHIT WE HAVE ANOTHER BROTHER! EVERYONE CHECK YOUR ACCOUNTS!"

The texts started buzzing—everyone was excited to meet the newest sibling. Jay and Briar were at a wedding, so neither of them had their phones on. I logged on to 23andMe, and there he was:

You have a new DNA relative.
Max G.: Half Brother. 23.4% DNA shared.

Everyone was writing to each other impatiently, trying to figure out who would reach out to Max first. I tried to be the voice of reason and suggested we elect one person in hopes of not overwhelming him. I was immediately shot down by my BioSibs, who were all eager to speak to Max. At least I tried.

We quickly learned that Max, like Liz and me, was a Long Islander. I decided I would wait until the morning to reach out, since I assumed having one less sibling to speak to might make it easier on him. By the end of that night, Jay and Briar turned their phones on to find the 50-something text messages they'd missed. Jay immediately sent a message to Max. He was now a pro at welcoming a new child.

The next morning, I reached out to Max to introduce myself and see how he was doing, knowing the night before, he was put into *his* Forever Haze of After. We hit it off right away. Max was stunned, anxious, nervous, and happy. I knew *exactly* how he felt. He couldn't believe that we were all so nice and willing to speak to him. I felt like I needed to be there for Max, just like Will had been there for me.

Max was nervous to speak to Jay and was overwhelmed by how fast everything was happening. By now, the rest of us BioSibs were so close, we assumed that any new sibling we'd find would want to jump right in. As much as Max did want to, it was still a lot to swallow.

Jay and Max spoke that day, and afterward, Max messaged me that he couldn't believe how cool Jay was. Once again, I knew *exactly* what he was feeling. Just like the BioSibs did for me, I talked to Max for a while to make sure he was okay. Jay invited Max to the award ceremony, but he was uncomfortable walking into a situation like that without knowing anyone.

I suggested to Max that since we lived only about an hour from each other, we should meet for lunch. This way when we got to the award ceremony, he would at least know me. Max appreciated my offer, and we set up a lunch date for the following month.

———

When Andrew and I showed up to meet Max and his fiancé for lunch, he immediately reminded us of Ari. There was something in their humor and personalities that was eerily similar, but I guess it wasn't that weird—since they are brothers.

Max told me his story, how he was raised by his mom and "god-mother," who he later found out was actually his mom's partner. He felt a connection to our sibling group, knowing that Sydney and Brit were in the same situation as his mom and her partner. Max always knew a dad wasn't in the picture, since he was raised by two women. He reached out to the donor agency and, like me, received minimal information about the donor. When his fiancé bought him the DNA test, he was hopeful he'd find siblings but never thought he'd find the donor himself.

Max was nervous to meet Jay but felt more comfortable doing so now that he at least had met me. We were looking forward to the award ceremony, and I couldn't wait to get together with even more of my BioSibs.

———

When the award ceremony weekend arrived, it was the first time I met Sydney, Brit, and my newborn niece, Thea. Just like the other first-time meetings, I felt like I had known them my whole life. Sydney has become one of my favorite people on the planet, and although we grew up completely opposite, we have a bond like we've been sisters our whole lives. She now has a newborn son, and she's one of those moms who make having two kids under two look easy. Sydney jokes that as a kid, she would ask Jay and Briar for older sisters, so she claims that she "willed us into existence."

Seeing Jay accept an award for his outstanding philanthropic contributions was a humbling experience. He gave a speech to the graduating class, and as I watched from the front row, I kept thinking, *I can't believe that man is my father*. I looked around the packed stadium in awe that all eyes were on him. People were so drawn into his story, his experience, and his success. I was proud to be his child.

Max couldn't make it to the award ceremony but met us the following day for lunch. Before we went up to Jay's hotel room, I met Max in the lobby to make sure he was okay. He assured me he was and said, "I know something in my life is about to happen. I'm just not sure what."

In my head I was thinking, *You're about to enter a Forever Haze of After, bro!*

The weekend was amazing. We all went out to dinner and laughed over a few beers. I looked around the table and couldn't believe I was sitting with my biological father and my brothers and sisters. It was awesome how well we all meshed and got along.

By this time, my grandma had become Facebook friends with Jay and most of my BioSibs, who coined her title, "BioGram." Grandma was so excited that not only was Jay a good man, he was a good Jewish man! One night when we were all hanging out in Jay's hotel suite, he asked me to call her, and when I did, he took the phone and walked away. About 15 minutes later he came back and handed me the phone. "Your grandma is such a nice lady! I really hope I can meet her one day. Make sure to call her later."

Jay and Briar told me how much they wanted to meet my mom and grandma and said the next time they were in New York they wanted to make sure that happened. I kept thinking how special a moment that could be.

Later that night I called my grandma and apologized about the surprise call from Jay. She said, "Oh, honey, don't apologize. Now I know what you mean. I spoke to him for 15 minutes but I feel like I've known him forever! He just has this way about him."

A few days after the weekend, Max sent a text out to the group saying he had such an incredible time, he and his fiancé had decided to invite all of us to their wedding, which was a few months away. That very night, Jay booked his flight to New York. Within weeks we learned that every one of us would be able to make it. It would be the first time that all nine siblings would be in the same place at once. Max would be meeting four of his siblings, Sabrina, Will, Jordan, and Eric, for the first time, on his wedding day.

———

Around the same time, Jay and Briar invited the BioSibs to join them on their annual family trip to Las Vegas and Zion National Park that summer. This was extra special to me, since my mom and I hadn't been able to afford a family vacation since I was six years old.

Max and Liz couldn't make it due to prior engagements, but the rest of us would be there. Spending time relaxing by the pool and hiking with my BioSibs was unforgettable. We bonded and spent most of the week laughing and comparing different traits. Jordan and I told Jay it was messed up that we were only 5'1" when Sabrina was 5'10". We compared how flat-footed we were and told Jay it was all his fault. He apologized for our genetic mutation and said, "At least I gave you good teeth!"

Jay told us that when he meets new patients, if they ask how many kids he has, his new line is "I have nine children with seven different women." We were all rolling on the floor laughing. I mean, he's not lying!

We realized that we'd all inherited Jay's neurotic list-making trait and were spooked when we noticed most of our calendars were weirdly color coordinated.

We learned that Jay was very close with his Uncle Will, and it was really special to Jay that one of his sons shared that name. We also learned that Ari's middle name was Max. *Weird!* We learned that Ari and Will share the same birthday, 11 years apart. We got to spend time with our newborn niece, Thea, and were happy to know that she would grow up in a family where she wasn't the only sperm-donor baby. All her aunts and uncles were too, thanks to her grandpa!

We got to bond with Briar and really see how much she loved and accepted us like her own children. When people hear our story, they don't understand *why* she opened her life up to us. To her, it's simple. We are her husband's children, and she loves us because we are good people who likewise care about them. Each of us, in our own way, reminds her of Jay. She knows our individual stories and always wanted a large family. Briar wanted six kids of her own, but sadly she had three miscarriages. She tells us, "You guys are the six kids I always wanted." Briar was a huge inspiration for me to write this book after I read her story in her recently published book, *Love, Laugh, Be: How I Wound Up with Nine Amazing Kids (When I Only Knew about Three) and Other Extraordinary True Stories That Matter.* I'm one of those kids!

When the trip was over, it was sad to say goodbye, but we would all be back together in a few months for Max's wedding. We couldn't wait for all nine of us to be together at once.

51

"MOM, MEET MY DAD"

Jay told me that since he'd be in New York for the wedding weekend, he thought it would be a perfect opportunity to meet my mom and grandma. The thought of them actually meeting each other was unbelievable to me. When I asked my mom and grandma how they felt about it, they both were equally excited and couldn't wait. They would also be meeting most of my BioSibs. We planned a brunch for that weekend.

As the wedding got closer, my mom remained excited but started feeling nervous. She couldn't believe that she was going to meet C380, the man behind the donor application, the man whose baby she carried for nine months.

My BioSibs would message my grandma on Facebook telling her how excited they were to meet BioGram. Brock and his wife had planned to meet at the hotel as well; they were going to be Thea's babysitters for the night while we were at the wedding. I couldn't believe my grandma, mom, biological father, and all of my siblings were going to be in the same place at once.

The night before the wedding, Sabrina and I had a slumber party and stayed up until 2 a.m. talking and laughing in our pajamas. It was wild to be with someone who was practically a stranger, but was my sister. We bonded deeply that night and our relationship has grown into one of the most genuine connections I've ever had.

The evening of the wedding was an absolute blast. We danced all night, laughed our asses off, and took a picture of all nine siblings in age order. It was such a special moment to be looking from side to side and seeing all my siblings. These people, whom I dreamt of and wrote about for years in my diary, questioning their existence—now they were here, right next to me.

We'd see other wedding guests whispering, "Are you guys the siblings? Is that Max's dad?" It was like without saying anything, they knew who we were. Maybe it was because of the dimple in all our chins.

The next day arrived and my mom and grandma headed to the hotel. When they got there, I met them outside while Jay, Briar, and my BioSibs waited in the lobby. My mom took a deep breath and said, "Okay, I'm ready."

Grandma walked in first and gave Jay and Briar hugs, thanking them repeatedly for being such good people. I loved that this was a moment I could share with my grandma. I was elated that she could finally see for herself that after all the worry I had for 10 years about my dad being a good man, here he was—and he wasn't good, he was the best.

My mom followed me in, and when she saw Jay, both of them got emotional. They were crying out of happiness and pride. My mom hugged Jay and kept saying, "Thank you. Thank you so much."

I couldn't believe that this moment was happening, that my mom was finally meeting the man who helped create me, who gave me 51 percent of my DNA. I had such a sense of completeness and fulfillment seeing them embrace, knowing that all the shit my mom and I had been through when I was growing up was in our past. This moment was the moment that mattered.

Seeing my mom and Jay together made me feel so happy for my mom. After all the bad shit that my dad put her through, she deserved to have a man like Jay be the father of her child.

I took a deep breath, and after they separated and wiped their tears away, I got to say something that most people in the world have never been able to say.

"Mom . . . meet my dad."

EPILOGUE

While this book was in its final stages of editing, my dad passed away from cancer. Initially, I wasn't sure if I should change parts of the book or leave them as they were. I ultimately decided to keep the book as it was originally written.

My relationship with my dad has been the biggest challenge of my life. I sometimes wish we could have gone back and started over. It hurts my heart to know that aside from his girlfriend, he didn't have any friends or family to surround him. At this point in our lives, Brock and I haven't seen him in almost a decade. This was an incredibly complicated situation for all of us.

I was happy to learn that my dad spent the past four years in an apparently "normal" relationship. I have never met his partner, but I've spoken to her often since his cancer diagnosis. She is a lovely person, and when she tells me about her relationship with my dad, I feel like I do not know the man she is speaking about. She didn't know his angry or unloving side; she describes a man who was caring and funny—a man I never knew. I hope, for his sake, he truly did experience love and happiness.

My dad's deficiencies were not mine, but the truth is, my relationship with him helped shape me into the woman I am today. For that, I am grateful. I am proud of the person I grew up to be, notwithstanding the struggles he and I experienced.

He wasn't a part of my life for much of his time here on Earth, but maybe he will watch me now and see how far I've come. I bet he'd be proud.

I hope and wish that my dad's soul is now at peace.

Rest in Peace, Dad
11/15/1954–11/22/2020

ACKNOWLEDGMENTS

This book would not have been possible without the support of my family and friends. I would not be the person I am if it weren't for you.

Self-Publishing School and my mentor, Ramy, thank you for holding my hand through this writing process. For keeping me accountable and teaching me how to make my dream a reality. My editor, Beth, thank you for elevating my story and helping me cross the finish line.

My best friends—Amanda, Rebekkah, Sam, and Jaclyn. Through it all, you have been my rocks. You have taught me that quality over quantity matters in friendships. You have picked me up at my worsts and stood next to me during my bests. I love you girls so much.

Jen, where do I begin? If it weren't for you, I don't know if I would have made it through my twenties. You have been my best friend since the day we sat at Jon's memorial site together over 13 years ago. Our relationship is one of my most treasured gems. Thank you so much for your help with life and your help with this book. LYPH.

Brock, my brother. You have been the main guy in my life since we were kids. I am beyond proud of the man you turned into, and I cherish our relationship. You are one of the smartest people I know and have the biggest heart. You have been and will always be one of my best friends.

Grandma, I can't imagine not having you to call every week. You are my constant source of wisdom and guidance. I usually don't make a decision without running it by you. Thank you for helping me through my childhood and remaining one of my closest friends. I love our relationship and I love you!

Mom, you are what all moms should strive to be. You taught me strength during weak times, you taught me hope during dark times, you taught me to be independent and to fight for what is right. You raised Brock and me to be caring, respectful, polite, driven, and loving. Some people thought we'd turn out differently, but you made sure we stayed on the right track, no matter how many curves life threw at us. You are my inspiration, and I love you. Thank you for helping me edit this book!

My BioSibs—you are my happy ending. Thank you for being you. Thank you for accepting me and loving me like we've known each other our whole lives. Thank you for letting me interview you for this book and taking time out to help me through this process. I can't wait to have a lifetime more of memories with you. Briar, thank you for pushing me to write this book and for my mini-therapy sessions. You are one of the kindest souls I've ever met.

Jay, I could never have dreamt my biological father would be someone like you. You have exceeded all expectations and embraced me as if you raised me. I can't thank you enough for opening your life to me and showing me what a dad should be like. I sometimes still cannot believe that I found you, but now that I have, I can't picture my life without you.

Lastly—my husband, Andrew. Our story may not have started out like a fairy tale, but it sure feels like one now. Thank you for pushing me to invest in myself and to write this book. Thank you for allowing me to share some of our darkest of times. Thank you for showing me every single day how much power and control someone has over their own life. Congratulations on six years of sobriety. I am beyond proud of you. I hope our story can help other couples struggling with addiction. I love you with every piece of my heart. Thank you for loving me back.

Every single person has experienced a moment that changed them forever. I hope you now can embrace your own Forever Haze of *After*.

If you are interested in learning more about the principled approach that transformed Andrew's life out of addiction, please visit www.centeredrecovery.com

ABOUT THE AUTHOR

Hilary Marsh was born and raised on Long Island. She and her husband, Andrew, enjoy traveling and experiencing different cultures and foods around the world. At 12 years old Hilary decided she would marry Andrew. At 17 she decided she would write a book about her life. At 20 she set out on a mission to find her biological father. By 32 she had accomplished it all, and more. Hilary currently works in title insurance by day and writes at night. She and Andrew live in Putnam County, New York, with their blue-nose pit bulls, Cayman and Oslo. *The Forever Haze of After* is her first book.

For more information, please visit
www.TheForeverHazeOfAfter.com
or contact Hilary at
TheForeverHazeOfAfter@gmail.com

CAN YOU HELP?

Thank You for Reading My Book!

I really appreciate all your feedback, and I love hearing what you have to say. Like most authors, I rely on online reviews to encourage future sales.

Please leave me an honest review on Amazon letting me know what you thought of the book.

Thanks so much!

Hilary Marsh

Made in the USA
Middletown, DE
20 July 2021